주한미군지위협정(SOFA)

서명 및 발효 16

주한미군지위협정(SOFA)

서명 및 발효 16

한국학술정보

| 머리말

미국은 오래전부터 우리나라 외교에 있어서 가장 긴밀하고 실질적인 우호 · 협력관계를 맺어온 나라다. 6 · 25전쟁 정전 협정이 체결된 후 북한의 재침을 막기 위한 대책으로서 1953년 11월 한미 상호방위조약이 체결되었다. 이는 미군이 한국에 주둔하는 법적 근거였고, 그렇게 주둔하게 된 미군의 시설, 구역, 사업, 용역, 출입국, 통관과 관세, 재판권 등 포괄적인 법적 지위를 규정하는 것이 바로 주한미군지위협정(SOFA)이다. 그러나 이와 관련한 협상은 계속된 난항을 겪으며 한미 상호방위조약이 체결로부터 10년이 훌쩍 넘은 1967년이 돼서야 정식 발효에 이를 수 있었다. 그럼에도 당시 미군 범죄에 대한 한국의 재판권은 심한 제약을 받았으며, 1980년대 후반 민주화 운동과 함께 미군 범죄 문제가 사회적 이슈로 떠오르자 협정을 개정해야 한다는 목소리가 커지게 되었다. 이에 1991년 2월 주한미군지위협정 1차 개정이 진행되었고, 이후에도 여러 사건이 발생하며 2001년 4월 2차 개정이 진행되어 현재에 이르고 있다.

본 총서는 외교부에서 작성하여 최근 공개한 주한미군지위협정(SOFA) 관련 자료를 담고 있다. 1953년 한미 상호방위조약 체결 이후부터 1967년 발효가 이뤄지기까지의 자료와 더불어, 이후 한미 합동위원회을 비롯해 민 · 형사재판권, 시설, 노무, 교통 등 각 분과위원회의 회의록과 운영 자료, 한국인 고용인 문제와 관련한 자료, 기타 관련 분쟁 자료 등을 포함해 총 42권으로 구성되었다. 전체 분량은 약 2만 2천여 쪽에 이른다.

2024년 3월

한국학술정보(주)

| 일러두기

· 본 총서에 실린 자료는 2022년 4월과 2023년 4월에 각각 공개한 외교문서 4,827권, 76만 여 쪽 가운데 일부를 발췌한 것이다.

· 각 권의 제목과 순서는 공개된 원본을 최대한 반영하였으나, 주제에 따라 일부는 적절히 변경하였다.

· 원본 자료는 A4 판형에 맞게 축소하거나 원본 비율을 유지한 채 A4 페이지 안에 삽입하였다. 또한 현재 시점에선 공개되지 않아 '공란'이란 표기만 있는 페이지 역시 그대로 실었다.

· 외교부가 공개한 문서 각 권의 첫 페이지에는 '정리 보존 문서 목록'이란 이름으로 기록물 종류, 일자, 명칭, 간단한 내용 등의 정보가 수록되어 있으며, 이를 기준으로 0001번부터 번호가 매겨져 있다. 이는 삭제하지 않고 총서에 그대로 수록하였다.

· 보고서 내용에 관한 더 자세한 정보가 필요하다면, 외교부가 온라인상에 제공하는 『대한민국 외교사료요약집』 1991년과 1992년 자료를 참조할 수 있다.

| 차례

정/리/보/존/문/서/목/록

기록물종류	문서-일반공문서철	등록번호	941 9614	등록일자	2006-07-27
분류번호	741.12	국가코드	US	주제	
문서철명	한.미국 간의 상호방위조약 제4조에 의한 시설과 구역 및 한국에서의 미국군대의 지위에 관한 협정 (SOFA) 전59권. 1966.7.9 서울에서 서명 : 1967.2.9 발효 (조약 232호) *원본				
생산과	미주과/조약과	생산년도	1952 - 1967	보존기간	영구
담당과(그룹)	조약	조약	서가번호	--	
참조분류					
권차명	V.43 SOFA 협정 체결교섭 관련 한.미국 교환문서집, 1953-59				
내용목차	* 일지 : 1953.8.7 이승만 대통령-Dulles 미국 국무장관 공동성명 - 상호방위조약 발효 후 군대지위협정 교섭 약속 1954.12.2 정부, 주한 UN군의 관세업무협정 체결 제의 1955.1월, 5월 미국, 제의 거절 1955.4.28 정부, 군대지위협정 제의 (한국측 초안 제시) 1957.9.10 Hurter 미국 국무차관 방한 시 각서 수교 (한국측 제의 수락 요구) 1957.11.13, 26 정부, 개별 협정의 단계적 체결 제의 1958.9.18 Dawling 주한미국대사, 형사재판관할권 협정 제외 조건으로 행정협정 체결 의사 전달 1960.3.10 정부, 토지, 시설협정의 우선적 체결 강력 요구 1961.4.10 장면 국무총리-McConaughy 주한미국대사 공동성명으로 교섭 개시 합의 1961.4.15, 4.25 제1, 2차 한.미국 교섭회의 (서울) 1962.3.12 정부, 교섭 재개 촉구 공한 송부 1962.5.14 Burger 주한미국대사, 최규하 장관 면담 시 형사재판관할권 문제 제기 않는 조건으로 교섭 재개 통고 1962.9.6 한.미국 간 공동성명 발표 (9월 중 교섭 재개 합의) 1962.9.20~1965.6.7 제1-81차 실무 교섭회의 (서울) 1966.7.8 제82차 실무 교섭회의 (서울) 1966.7.9 서명 1967.2.9 발효 (조약 232호)					

마/이/크/로/필/름/사/항

촬영연도	*롤 번호	화일 번호	후레임 번호	보관함 번호
2006-11-24	I-06-0071	03	1-155	

0001

CONTENTS

0002

0003

0004

1. Statement by President Rhee and Secretary of State Dulles, August 7, 1953.

Our friendly and understanding consultations demonstrate clearly the determination of the United States and the Republic of Korea to stand together in cordial cooperation to achieve our common objectives, including the reunification of Korea.

We have today initialed a draft of a mutual-defense treaty. That treaty is designed to unite our nations in common action to meet common danger and it will cement the ties which have brought us together to combat in Korea the menace of Communist aggression.

Our two governments will actively proceed with the constitutional processes necessary to bring this treaty into full forces and effect. These constitutional processes, in the case of the United States, require that the United States Senate consent to the ratification. The United States Senate, having adjourned this week, will not again be in regular session until next January. However, United States Senate leaders have been kept fully informed of the exchange of views which have led to the action we have taken today and it is

미문84-1(5)

0006

~~0007~~

our sincere hope that this will lead to prompt and favorable United States Senate action.

Between now and the date when the Mutual Defense Treaty can be expected to come into force and effect, our armed forces in Korea will be subject to the United Nations Command which will comply with the armistice terms. If, during this period, there should occur unprovoked armed attack by the Communist forces against the Republic of Korea in violation of the armistice, the UNC, including the Republic of Korea forces, would at once and automatically react, as such an unprovoked attack would be an attack upon and a threat to the UNC itself and to the forces under its command. Such reaction to an un-provoked armed attack would not be a new war but rather a resumption by the Communist forces of the active belligerency which the armistice has halted.

The UNC will be constantly alert against such an attack.

Our Government will promptly negotiate agreements to cover the status of such forces as the United States may elect to maintain in Korea after the mutual-defense treaty comes into force and effect, and the availability

0007 ~~0008~~

~~0006~~

미.무 84-1

0008

~~0009~~

to them of Korean Facilities and services will continue as at present.

The armistice comtemplates that a political conference will be convened within three months, that is, prior to October 27, 1953. At that conference the United States delegation, in cooperation with the ROK delegation, and other delegations from the UNC side, will seek to achieve the peaceful unification of historic Korea as a free and independent nation. We and our advisers have already had a full and satisfactory exchange of views which we hope and trust will establish a preparatory foundation for coordinated effort at the political conference.

If, after the political conference has been in session for 90 days, it becomes clear to each of our governments that all attempts to achieve these objectives have been fruitless and that the confernce is being exploited by the Communist delegates mainly to infiltrate, propagandize or otherwise embarrass the Republic of Korea, we shall then be prepared to make a concurrent withdrawal from the conference. We will then consult further regarding the attainment of a unified, free and

0009

0010

미운84-1

0010

~~0011~~

결 번

넘버링 오류

independent Korea which is the postwar goal the United States set itself during World War II, which has been accepted by the United Nations as its goal and which will continue to be an object of concern of United States Foreign policy.

We recognize that the Republic of Korea possesses the inherent right of sovereignty to deal with its problems, but is has agreed to take no unilateral action to unite Korea by military means for the agreed duration of the political conference.

We contemplate that the projected three to four year program for the rehabilitation of the war ruined Korean economy shall be coordinated through the combined economic board, under the joint chairmanship of the Korean and American representatives. This program contemplates the expenditure of approximately one billion dollars of funds, subject to appropriations thereof by the United States Congress. Two hundred million dollars has already been authorized, out of prospective defense savings.

We have exchanged preliminary views with respect

0012

to various problems involving the maintenance and development of ROK land, air and sea forces.

We feel confident that the relationship thus established between our two governments marks an important contribution to the developing of independence and freedom in the Far East. With unshaking faith in the principle of collective security, and with loyal adherence to the Charter of the United Nations, we intend to move forward together toward the achievement of our common objective - the restoration of a unified, democratice and independent Korean nation.

There are no other agreements or understandings stated or implied resulting from these consultations other than those herein contained.

0013

미문811-1(5)

0014

2. Acting Foreign Minister's letter of December 2, 1954 to the United States Ambassador, and the enclosed Draft Agreement regarding custom's functions with respect to the United Nations Forces in Korea.

December 2, 1954

My dear Ambassador:

I have the honour of writing to you concerning a conclusion of provisional agreement regarding the functions of Korean customs' authorities with respect to the United Nations forces in Korea.

For some years, we have a serious problem of various luxury goods and other items that have been pouring into our country from abroad through some illegal means, and they are flooded throughout the country, thus creating one cause of greatly damaging effects to our economy. An effective measure to be agreed upon between the Korean Government and the United Nations Command to regulate lawful entry of goods from abroad will contribute, in no small way, toward the sound economy of Korea absolutely desirable at this time of rehabilitation.

駐韓 UN軍을 規律하는 잠정 관세협정의 체결을 제의하는 조외무차관의 Briggs 주한미대사앞 서한 및 동 초안 (54.12.2)

54-10-10(16) 비문 04-2(16)

0016

There exists, for some time, a strong opinion among the people and the Government circle that demands the desirability of concluding an Agreement defining the relationship between the Government of the Republic of Korea and the United Nations forces in regard to the former's customs' functions. Such an Agreement will remain in force pending conclusion of a General Administrative Agreement which shall cover other subjects also.

In the belief that a conclusion of the Agreement is in the mutual interests, I wish to propose formally, on behalf of the Korean Government, that negotiation be commenced between the representatives of my Government and the Unified Command. Upon the receipt of your consent, we shall appoint our representatives, and shall also suggest a date and place of the conference which will be mutually agreeable.

Accept, My dear Ambassador, the assurnaces of my highest consideration.

C. W. Cho
Acting Minister

0017

14-11-75

미문94-2

0018

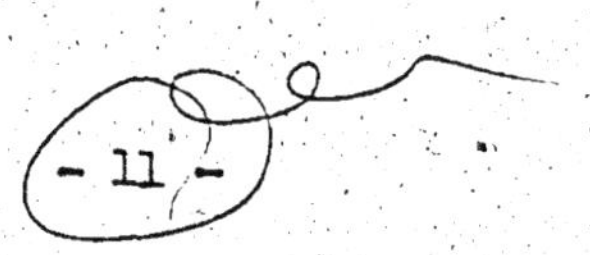

His Excellency

Ellis C. Briggs

Ambassador of the United States

Seoul.

0019

54-11-96

미·문 84-2

0020

DRAFT AGREEMENT REGARDING CUSTOMS' FUNCTIONS
WITH RESPECT TO THE UNITED NATIONS FORCES IN KOREA

WHEREAS the United Nations forces are engaged in action in Korea pursuant to the Security Council Resolutions of June 25, June 27 and July 7, 1950 and the General Assembly Resolution of February 1, 1951, which called upon all States and authorities to lend every assistance to the United Nations action;

WHEREAS the Republic of Korea has been and is rendering utmost cooperation to the forces which are participating in the United Nations action in Korea;

WHEREAS the United Nations forces import into and export from Korea a large amount of materials, supplies and equipment, consequence of which necessitates definition of relationship between the Government of the Republic of Korea and the United Nations forces with respect to the former's customs' functions; and

WHEREAS it is considered naturally desirable to conclude a provisional Agreement regarding the said customs' functions pending conclusion of general Administrative Agreement between the Government of the

0021

84-11-177

Republic of Korea and the Governments of the States sending forces to Korea pursuant to the United Nations Resolutions;

NOW, THEREFORE, the Parties to this Agreement have agreed as follows:

ARTICLE I

In this Agreement the expression:

(a) "Parties to this Agreement" means the Government of the Republic of Korea, the Government of the United States of America acting as the Unified Command, and each Government which signs or accedes to, this Agreement, as the Government of a State which has sent or may hereafter send forces to Korea pursuant to the United Nations Resolutions.

(b) "United Nations forces" means those forces of the land, sea or air armed services of the States which are sent to Korea to engage in action pursuant to the United Nations Resolutions.

(c) "Members of the United Nations forces" means personnel on active duty belonging to the United Nations forces when such persons are in Korea.

0022

54-11-78

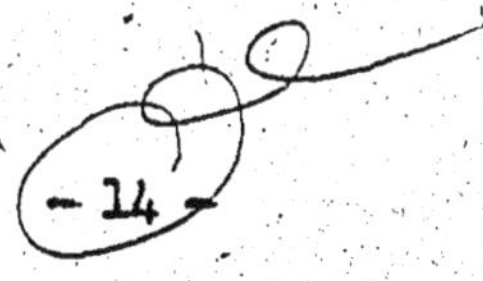

(d) "Civilian component" means the civilian persons of the nationality of any State sending forces to Korea pursuant to the United Nations Resolutions who are in the employ of the United Nations forces when such persons are in Korea, but excludes persons who are ordinarily resident in Korea.

(e) "Dependents" means the following persons, when such persons are in Korea:

(i) Spouse, and children under 21, of members of the United Nations forces or of the civilian component;

(ii) Parents, and children over 21, of members of the United Nations forces or of the civilian components, if dependent for over half their support upon such members.

ARTICLE II

Save as provided to the contrary in this Agreement, members of the United Nations forces, the civilian component, and their dependents shall be

0024

54-11-11P →

미·문84-2
0025

subject to the laws and regulations administered by the customs authorities of Korea.

ARTICLE III

The United Nations forces or the non-appropriated fund organizations authorized and regulated by such forces including navy exchanges, post exchanges, messes, social clubs, theatres and newspapers may import free of duty all materials, supplies and equipment, exclusively for the official use of the United Nations forces or for the use of the members of the United Nations forces, the civilian component, and their dependents. The duty-free importation shall be verified bya certificate issued by the United Nations authorities in a form agreed between Korea and the United Nations forces.

ARTICLE IV

Property consigned to and for the personal use of members of the United Nations forces, the civilian component, and their dependents, shall be subject to customs duties, except that no duties shall

t4-11-80

0026

미·문84-2
0027

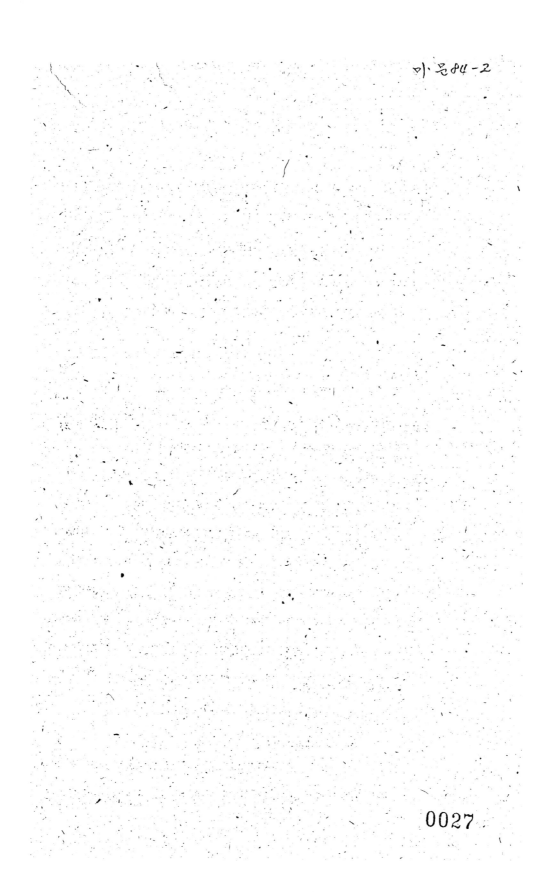

be paid with respect to:

(a) Furniture, household goods and other personal effects for their private use imported by the members of the United Nations forces civilian component, and their dependents at the time of their first arrival in Korea;

(b) Reasonable quantities of clothing and household goods of a type which would ordinarily be purchased in their home States for everyday use for the private use of members of the United Nations forces, civilian component, and their dependents, which are mailed into Korea through the United Nations military post offices.

ARTICLE V

Official documents under official seal and mail in the United Nations military postal channels shall not be subject to customs inspection.

ARTICLE VI

5411-81 0038

Goods which have been imported duty-free under Article III and IV above:

(a) may be re-exported freely, provided that, in the case of goods imported under Article III, a certificate is issued by the United Nations forces;

(b) shall not normally be disposed of in Korea by way of either sale or gift. However, in particular cases such disposal may be authorized on consitions agreed between the authorities of Korea and the United Nations forces.

ARTICLE VII

Exportation and re-importation of goods purchased in Korea shall be subject to the regulation in force in Korea. Such goods shall be regarded exported when deposited in a warehouse and deemed imported when removed from the warehouse.

ARTICLE VIII

In Article III, IV and VI of this Agreement,

54-11-83 0030

미.통84-2

0031

"duty" means customs duties and all other duties and taxes payable on importation or exportation, as the case may be, except dues and taxes which are no more than charges for services rendered.

ARTICLE IX

1. The customs authorities of Korea shall have the right, when desirable, in cooperation with the authorities of the United Nations forces to search members of the United Nations forces or civilian component and their dependents and examine their luggage and vehicles, and to seize articles pursuant to the laws and regulations administered by the customs authorities of Korea.

2. In order to prevent offenses against customs and fiscal laws and regulations, the authorities of Korea and of the United Nations shall assist each other in the conduct of inquiries and the collection of evidence.

3. The authorities of the United Nations forces shall render all assistance within their power to ensure that articles liable to seizure by, or on behalf

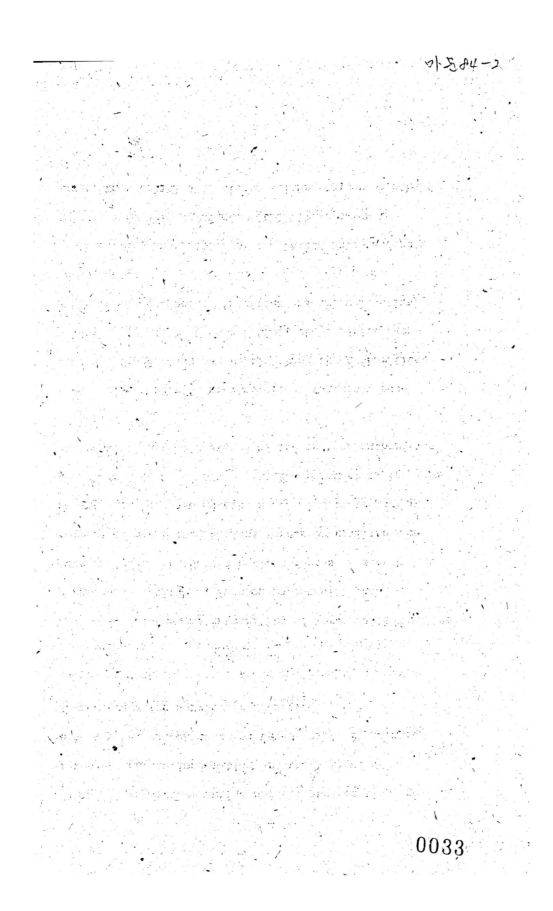

of, the customs or fiscal authorities of Korea are handed to those authorities.

4. The authorties of the United Nations forces shall render all assistance within their power to ensure payment of duties, taxes and penalties payable by members of the United Nations forces or civilian component or their dependents.

ARTICLE X

The Parties to this Agreement shall as promptly as possible take legislative, budgetary and other measures neces ary for the implimentation of this Agreement.

ARTICLE XI

1. A Joint Board shall be established in Seoul as the means for consultation and agreement between the Government of Korea and the other Parties to this Agreement on matters relating to the interpretation of this Agreement.

2. The Joint Board shall be composed of two

...

0034

representatives, one representing the Government of Korea and the other representing the other Parties to this Agreement, such of whom shall have one or more deputies and a staff. The Joint Board shall determine its own procedures, and arrange for such auxillary organs and administrative services as may be required. The Joint Board shall be so organized that it may meet at any time at the request of either representative.

3. If the Joint Board is unable to reach agreement on any matter, it shall be settled through intergovernmental negotiations.

ARTICLE XII

This Agreement shall come into forces on the date of signature by the representatives of the Government of Korea, the Government of the United States of America acting as the Unified Command, and the Governments of States having sent forces to Korea pursuant to the United Nations Resolutions.

ARTICLE XIII

5.4-11-86

0036

1. After the entry into force of this Agreement in accordance with Article XII, the Government of any State which hereafter sends forces to Korea pursuant to the United Nations Resolutions shall accede to this Agreement by depositing its instrument of accession with the Government of Korea.

2. The Government of Korea shall notify such Government which is already a Party to this Agreement, of the date of deposit of each instrument of accession.

3. This Agreement shall enter into force for each acceding Government ten days after the date of deposit of its instrument of accession.

ARTICLE XIV

Each Party may at any time request the revision of any Article of this Agreement. The request shall be addressed to the Joint Board.

ARTICLE XV

This Agreement and agreed revisions thereof shall terminate on the date by which all the United

0038

64-11-87

0039

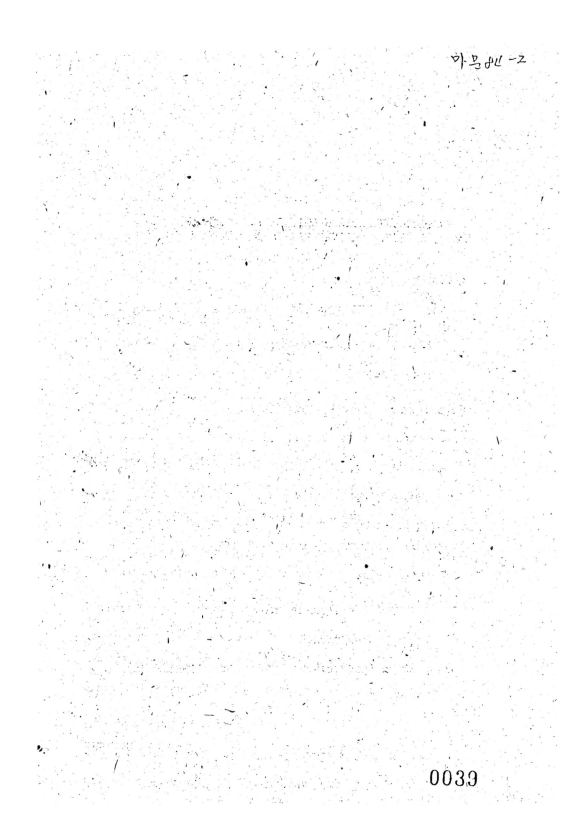

Nations forces shall be withdrawn from Korea, and shall resume its force automatically whenever such forces return to Korea.

IN WITNESS WHEREOF the undersigned, being duly authorized by their respective Governments for the purpose, have signed this Agreement.

DONE at Seoul this day of 1954 in the Korean and English languages, both texts being equally authoritative, in a single original which shall be deposited in the archives of the Government of Korea. The Government of Korea shall transmit certified copies thereof to all the signatory and acceding Governments.

For the Government of the Republic of Korea:

For the Government of the United States of America acting as the Unified Command:

GOVERNMENTS OF STATES SENDING FORCES TO KOREA PURSUANT TO THE UNITED NATIONS RESOLUTIONS

54-11.88

0040

For the Government of the Comm[illegible]h of Australia:

For the Government of Belgium:

For the Government of Canada:

For the Government of Colombia:

For the Government of Ethiopia:

For the Government of France:

For the Government of Greece:

For the Government of Italy:

For the Government of Netherlands:

For the Government of New Zealand:

For the Government of Norway:

For the Government of the Republic of Philippines:

For the Government of Thailand:

For the Government of Turkey:

For the Government of the Union of South Africa:

For the Government of the United Kingdom of
Great Britain and Northern Ireland:

0042

3. United States Ambassador's reply of January 27, 1955 to the Acting Foreign Minister's letter of December 2, 1954.

American Embassy,
Seoul, Korea,
January 27, 1955.

My dear Dr. Pyun:

On December 6, 1954, The Embassy received a letter from the Acting Minister of Foreign Affairs, dated December 2, 1954, concerning the possibility of negotiating an agreement with the United States defining the relationship between the Government of the Republic of Korea and the United Nations forces in regard to the former's customs functions. The Acting Minister enclosed a draft to form a basis of possible discussions.

This matter was already under study at General Hull's headquarters when the Acting Minister's letter was received at the Embassy. I am advised that General Hull informed you in a letter dated December 3, 1954, that he had directed that the entire matter be studied with a view to promulgating uniform procedures which will provide the Korean Customs officials an improved

0043

55-3-1 (2)

미·무 84-3(2)

0044

and reasonable opportunity to exercise their responsibility. I am pleased to be able to inform you that you will receive copies of the regulations covering these new procedures in the near future. I hope that you will find that they meet the requirements of the Government of the Republic of Korea without the necessity of negotiating a formal agreement, particularly since it will be possible to put them in effect as soon as they are completed.

I am, my dear Mr. Minister,

Sincerely yours,

/s/

Ellis O. Briggs
American Ambassador

His Excellency
Pyun Yung-tai,
Minister of Foreign Affairs of
the Republic of Korea.

55-8-2

0045

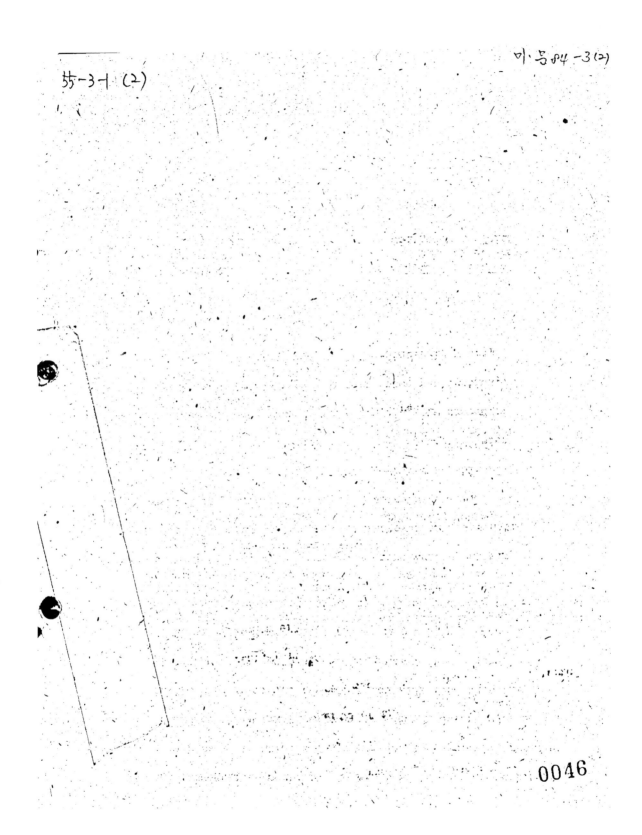

4. General Maxwell D. Taylor's letter of May 14, 1955 to the Foreign Minister.

14 May 1955

Dear Mr. Prime Minister:

In his letter to you of 3 December 1954, General Hull informed you that study was being given to the development of procedures under which Korean customs officials would be accorded an improved and reasonable opportunity to exercise their responsibilities.

I have recently approved a procedure which I feel will accomplish this objective, a copy of which is forwarded for your information. The new procedure goes into effect forty-five days after publication.

Sincerely yours,

/s/

MAXWELL D. TAYLOR
General, U. S. Army
Commander in Chief

I inclosure
Letter, this Headquarters, 14 May 55

0047

0048

His Excellency
Y. T. Pyun
Minister of Foreign Affairs
of the Republic of Korea
Seoul, Korea

0049

미문84-

0050

(Inclosure)

HEADQUARTERS
FAR EAST COMMAND
APO 500

AGJ 000.5 EJ/C 14 May 1955

SUBJECT: Controls Concerning Property Brought into Korea by Individuals

TO: Commanding General, United States Army Forces, Far East and Eighth United States Army, APO 343
Commander Naval Forces, Far East, c/o FPO San Francisco, California
Commander, Far East Air Forces, APO 925

1. Rescission: Letter, AGJ 000.5 EJ/C, Hq Far East Command, 6 December 1954, subject: "Establishment of Enforcement Procedure to Detect Smuggling in Korea."

2. Individuals, subject to the military jurisdiction of a force which has been sent by any State prusuant to Security Council and General Assembly resolutions which called upon all States to lend every assistance to the United Nations action in Korea, shall be permitted to bring into Korea, free from customs duties and other such charges, only reasonable quantities of privately

0051

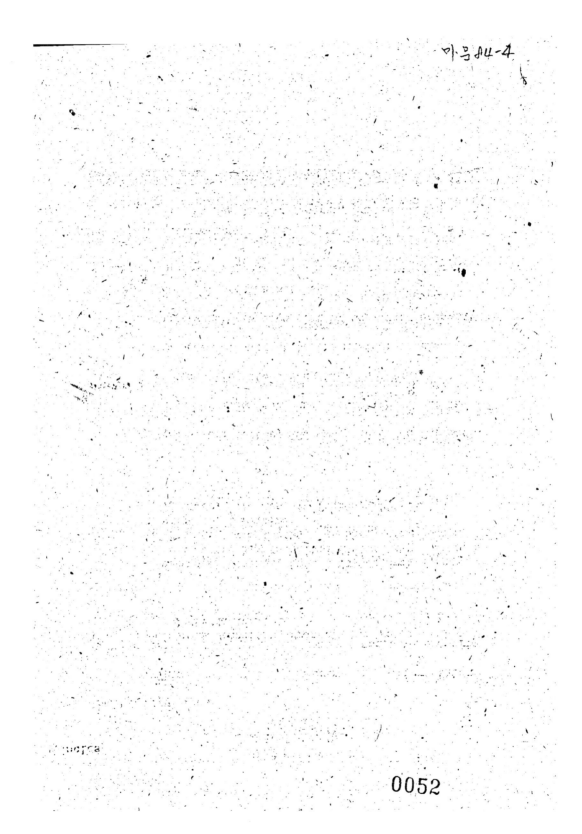

owned property for personal or family use; provided that the possession or entry into Korea of such property does not otherwise violate force, service or command regulations.

3. These instructions implement the policy stated above by establishing procedures with respect to property brought into Korea by individuals entering the country, where the entry of the individual and his accompanying baggage is by means of United States military transportation. The procedures will come into force and effect forty-five days following the publication date of this letter.

a. The Commander, Far East Air Forces, shall assume responsibility for the enforcement of the procedures at ports of entry under the jurisdiction of the Far East Air Forces.

b. The Commanding General, United States Army Forces, Far East and Eighth United States Army, shall assume responsibility for the enforcement of the procedures at other United States areas and facilities.

c. The Commanding General, United States Army Forces, Far East and Eighth United States Army, is

0053

미국84-4
0054

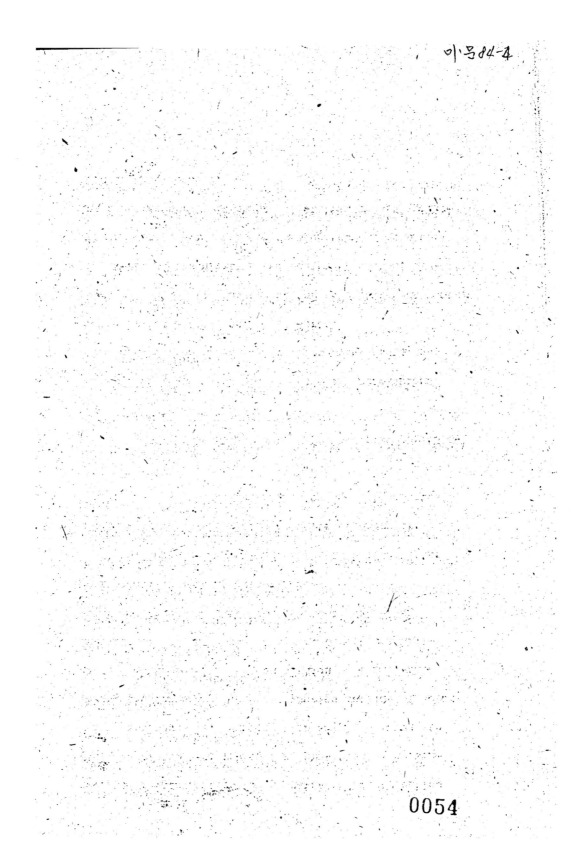

assigned responsibility for printing and distributing supplies of the declaration form provided for hereinbelow (Inclosure 1). Consideration should be given to making the forms available to agencies outside of Korea so as to make possible the completion of forms while individuals are on route to Korea. Direct communication to accomplish distribution and to establish appropriate liaison is authorized.

4. Individuals entering Korea by United States military transportation through ports of entry or facilities operated or controlled by the UnitedStates forces, shall be grouped as follows:

a. Persons subject to the military jurisdiction of a force which has been sent by any State prusuant to Security Council and General Assembly resolutions which called upon all States to lend every assistance to the United Nations action in Korea.

(1) Not travelling as a component member of a table of organization and equipment unit or provisional unit, which unit or portion thereof is entering Korea on permanent change of station orders applicable to unit members.

0055

미·은 84-4

0056

(2) Travelling as a component member of a table of organization and equipment unit or provisional unit, which unit or portion thereof is entering Korea on permanent change of station orders applicable to unit members.

b. Persons not subject to the military jurisdiction of a force which has been sent by any State pursuant to Security Council and General Assembly resolutions which called upon all States to lend every assistance to the United Nations action in Korea.

c. Persons not subject to military jurisdiction, paragraph 4b above, but entitled to special treatment because of their status (very important persons, diplomatic personnel, and similar categories).

5. When persons identified in paragraph 4a(1) above enter Korea through ports of entry or facilities operated or controlled by the United States forces:

a. Each individual shall complete and immediately upon or following debarkation submit to the United States forces port authorities in triplicate a declaration form.

b. This declaration form, Inclosure 1, shall

미·응 84-4

0058

be used to describe the privately owned property being brought into Korea by the declarant (property carried in by the individual, held or other baggage arriving with the individual, and other property held at the port awaiting the arrival of the individual). Military equipment and supplies which have been issued to or purchased by a declarant will not be listed or described in the declaration form. Reasonable quantities of privately owned personal effects, owned by and being brought into Korea for the personal use of the declarant, or for the use of a member of the family of the person making the declaration, may be described as "personal effects and clothing," without further detailed description, except that all items of property identified by serial numbers (expensive cameras, etc.) must be itemized and described separately.

c. Upon receipt, port authorities shall take the following actions concerning the declarant, the declaration form, and the property of each individual at the port of entry:

(1) United States forces authorities will review forms presented by individuals subject to United

마음84-4

0060

States court-martial jurisdiction and conduct spot checks or examinations of hand carried and other baggage or property at the port, noting on thedeclaration forms, that such spot checks or examinations have been accomplished. The examination may be similar to checks or inspections conducted by customs authorities. One copy of the noted form shall be returned to the declarant. One copy of the noted form shall be forwarded immediately to the nearest customs office of the Korean Government. In the event a spot check or examination results in the location of contraband property or items in excess of usual requirements, contraband and items identified as in excess of usual requirements shall be segregated from the other property of the individual concerned. Disposition of the property so segregated, and actions taken with respect to an individual who has attempted to bring into Korea the segregated items, shall be pursuant to applicable service or command regulations. Where segregated property has been or is to be disposed of pursuant to applicable service or command regulations, the copy of the declaration form forwarded to the Korean Customs office shall include remarks as to the property

0061

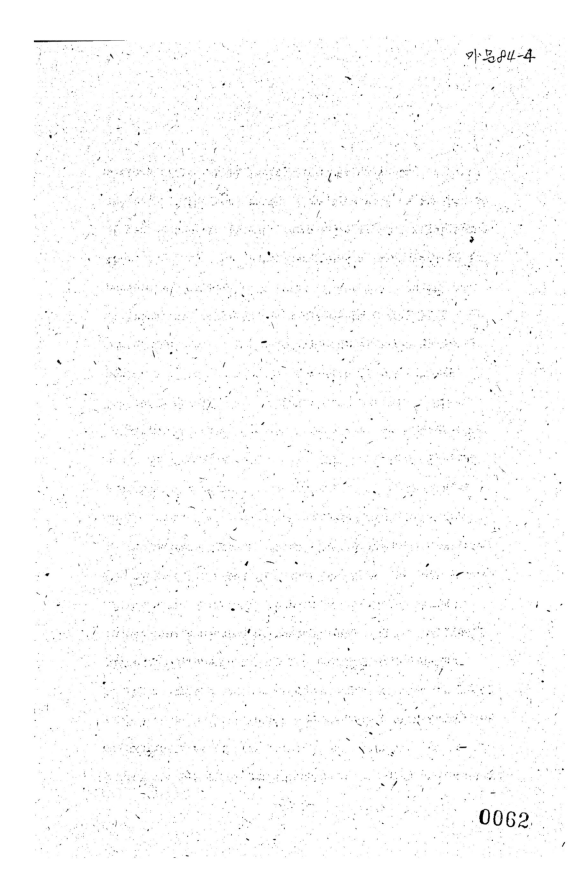

segregated and as to its disposition or pending disposition.

(2) When persons, identified in paragraph 4a(1), above, not subject to United States courts-martial jurisdiction, arrive in Korea, United States forces authorities shall channel such persons and the declaration forms presented by them to the representative at the port of the force which has jurisdiction over such individuals. As requested, United States forces authorities shall assist this force representative, in actions taken by the representative similar to the spot chechs or examinations discussed above. If there is no representative at the port of the force which has jurisdiction over an individual:

(a) Local United States military authorities may act for such force in the spot check or examination at the request of appropriate authorities of the concerned force.

(b) The individual and his property and baggage may be provided transportation to the nearest unit of the force to the port, for spot check or examination by competentofficials of the force.

0063

0064

(c) As requested by the appropriate authorities of the concerned force, the spot check or examination may be deferred until the arrival at the port of entry of a force representative.

6. Persons identified in paragraph 4a(2) above will not be required to complete or submit Inclosure 1, except at the direction of the officer in charge of the unit.

7. When persons identified in paragraph 4b above enter Korea through ports of entry or facilities operated or controlled by the United States forces, it shall be the responsibility of the United States military authorities of the concerned port of entry or facility to turn over such individuals and their property and baggage to the nearest Korean Government customs office immediately following the debarkation of the individual from the aircraft or vessel.

8. When persons identified in paragraph 4c above enter Korea through ports of entry or facilities operated or controlled by the United States forces, such persons shall be placed in touch with representatives of

0065

미·북84-4

0066

an appropriate agency or government in Korea, and actions with respect to clearing such personnel and their property and baggage into Korea through Korean Customs shall be the responsibility of such representatives.

9. The procedures stated above do not limit or restrict usual law enforcement activities, or additional measures taken separately or in cooperation with Korean officials designed to prevent or detect smuggling or the introduction of contraband property into Korea.

BY COMMAND OF GENERAL TAYLOR:

/s/
C.W. NELSON
Colonel, AGC
Adjutant General

1 Incl
Declaration Form

0067

마므 84-4(11)

0068

5. Foreign Minister's reply of June 13, 1955 to General Taylor's letter of May 14, 1955.

June 13, 1955

Dear General Lemnitzer:

I have the honour to acknowledge the receipt of the letter of May 14, 1955 signed by General Maxwell D. Taylor, then-Commander in Chief of the United Nations Command enclosing a copy of the letter AGJ 000.5 KJ/C signed by Colonel C.W. Nelson of the Headquarters of the same Command, the subject of which reads "Controls concerning Property Brought into Korea by Individuals".

The Ministry has taken note of the procedures described in the enclosed letter signed by Colonel Nelson.

While appreciating the voluntary cooperation on the part of the Command with respect to customs functions of the Republic of Korea, I wish to inform you of the desire of the Korean Government to commence negotiation with the Government of the United States, as soon as possible, for the conclusion of a comprehensive agreement between the Republic of Korea and the Unified Command regarding the status of the United Nations forces in Korea, etc., which will also define the customs functions

0069

미용84-5(2)

0070

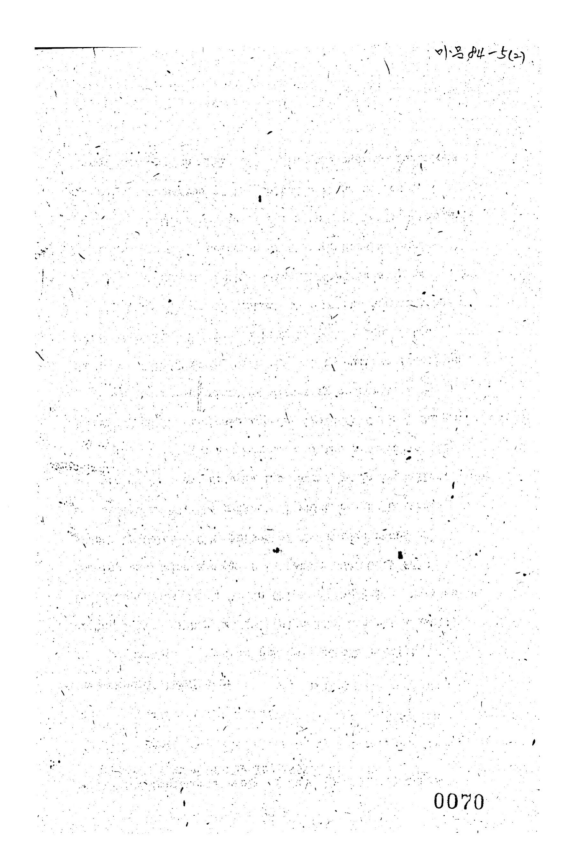

of the Korean Government, as already proposed in my letter of April 25, 1955 addressed to Mr. Carl W. Strom, Charge d'Affaires of the Embassy of the United States in Seoul, to which you can easily refer, if you think it advisable.

Y. T. Pyun
Minister

General Lyman L. Lemnitzer
Commander in Chief,
United Nations Command,
Tokyo, Japan

0071

미문84-5(2)

0072

6. Foreign Minister's letter of April 28, 1955 to the United States Charge d'Affaires, and the enclosed Draft Administrative Agreement proposed by ROK Government.

April 28, 1955

Dear Mr. Charge d'Affaires:

I have the honour to initiate a proposal to conclude an Administrative Agreement between the Government of the Republic of Korea and the Government of the United States of America, and enclose herewith a draft of the Agreement. With regard to this proposal, I would like first to refer to my note dated December 2, 1954, concerning a conclusion of provisional Agreement regarding the functions of Korean customs authorities with respect to the United Nations forces in Korea. Particular reference was made in the note to the effect that such customs agreement will remain in force pending conclusion of a General Administrative Agreement which shall cover other subjects also.

Having in mind that the United Nations forces under the Unified Command are and will be disposed in and about the territory of the Republic of Korea until the objective of the United Nations in Korea will have

0073

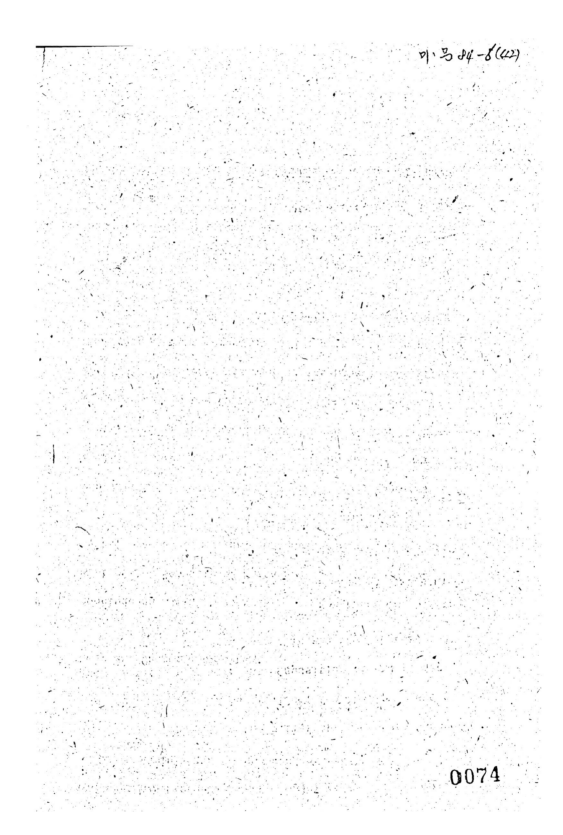

been achieved pursuant to the resolutions of the United Nations Security Council of June 25, 1950, June 27, 1950 and July 7, 1950, it is the belief of the Korean Government that terms shall be provided, for the interests of both parties, to govern the disposition of and render convenience to the said forces in and about Korea, and that they shall be determined through mutual agreement between the Republic of Korea and the United States of America acting as the Unified Command in accordance with "The Resolution on the Settlement of the Unified Command" if the Security Council of the United Nations of July 7, 1950. A practical and effective Administrative Agreement to be concluded between the said two parties will help minimize misunderstanding and maximize cooperativeness between the Korean people and United Nations forces personnel in Korea.

In the belief that a conclusion of the Agreement is in the mutual interests, I wish to propose formally, on behalf of the Government of the Republic of Korea, that negotiation will be commenced between the representatives of Korean Government and the United States Government. Upon the receipt of your consent, we will proceed

0075

미문84-6

0076

to decide the date and place of the conference, which will be mutually agreeable.

Accept, dear Mr. Charge d'Affaires, the assurnaces of my highest consideration.

Enclosure: Draft of Administrative
Agreement

/s/

Y. T. PYUN
Minister of Foreign
Affairs

The Honourable Carl W. Strom,
Charge d'Affaires,
Embassy of the United States of America
Seoul, Korea

0077

마드84-6
0078

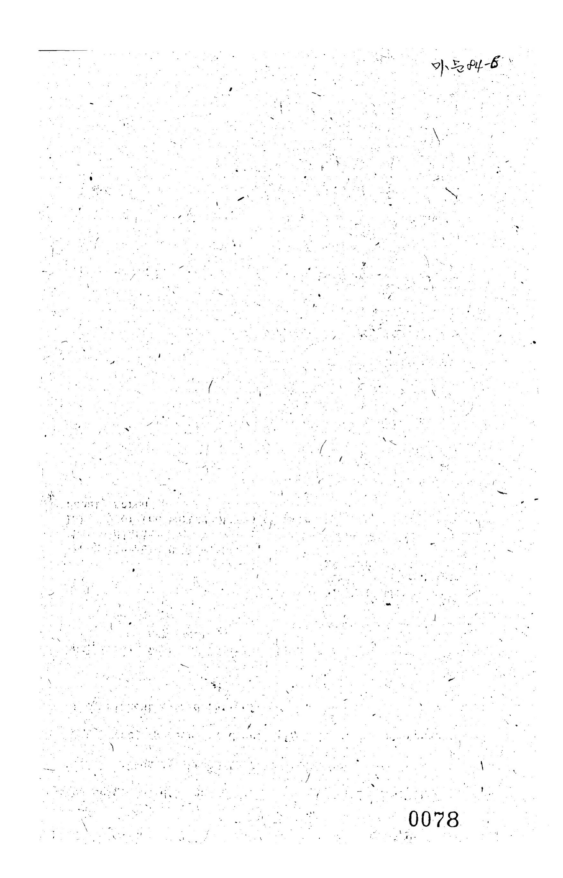

(Enclosure)

ADMINISTRATIVE AGREEMENT
BETWEEN THE REPUBLIC OF KOREA AND THE UNIFIED COMMAND
REGARDING THE STATUS OF THE UNITED NATIONS FORCES IN
KOREA

PREAMBLE

Mindful that the United Nations Forces under the Unified Command are disposed in and about the territory of the Republic of Korea pursuant to the resolutions of the United Nations Security Council of June 25, 1950, June 27, 1950 and July 7, 1950;

Considering that active hostilities in Korea have ceased with the conclusion of Armistice Agreement signed on July 27, 1953, alleviating the emergent conditions incident to military operations, and that the United Nations Forces will remain in and about the territory of the Republic of Korea until the objectives of the United Nations in Korea will have been achieved;

Believing that the conditions that shall govern the disposition of the United Nations Forces in and about the territory of the Republic of Korea should be determined by mutual agreement between the Republic of Korea and

0079

0080

the Unified Command;

And regarding it necessary that the Republic of Korea and the Unified Command conclude practical administrative arrangements which will help minimize misunderstanding and maximize cooperativeness between Korean people and United Nations Forces personnel in Korea hereunder specified;

Therefore, the Governments of the Republic of Korea and of the United States of America acting as the Unified Command have entered into this Agreement in terms as set forth below:

ARTICLE I

In this Agreement the expression:

(a) "members of the United Nations Forces" means the personnel on active duty belonging to the land, sea or air armed services under the Unified Command when in the territory of the Republic of Korea (hereinafter referred to as Korea) in connection with their official duties.

(b) "Civilian component" means the civilian personnel of the nationality of any state sending forces under

기.문84-6

0082

the Unified Command accompanying the United Nations forces who are in the employ of such forces in Korea. For the prupose of this Agreement only, dual nationals, Korean and of any state sending forces under the Unified Command who are brought to Korea by the United Nations forces shall be deemed as nationals of such state.

(c) "dependents" means

(i) spouse, and children under 21;

(ii) parents, and children over 21, if dependent for over half their support upon a member of the United Nations forces or civilian component.

ARTICLE II

1. Members of the United Nations forces shall be exempt from Korean passport and visa laws and regulations. Members of the United Nations forces, the civilian component, and their dependents shall be exempt from Korean laws and regulations on the registration and control of aliens, but shall not be considered as acquiring any right to permanent residence or domicile

0083

0084

in the territories of Korea.

2. Members of the United Nations forces shall be in possession of thefollowing documents upon entry into or departure from Korea:

(a) personal identity card issued by the United Nations forces authorities showing names, date of birth, rank and number, service and photograph;

(b) individual or collective movement order issued by the United Nations forces authorities and certifying to the status of the individual or group as a member or members of the United Nations forces and to the movement ordered.

For the purpose of identification while in Korea, members of the United Nations forces shall be in possession of the foregoing personal identity card.

3. Members of the civilian component, their dependents, and the dependents of the members of the United Nations forces shall be in possession of passports with their status described therein, upon their entry into or departure from Korea, and while in Korea.

0085

마-분84-6
0086

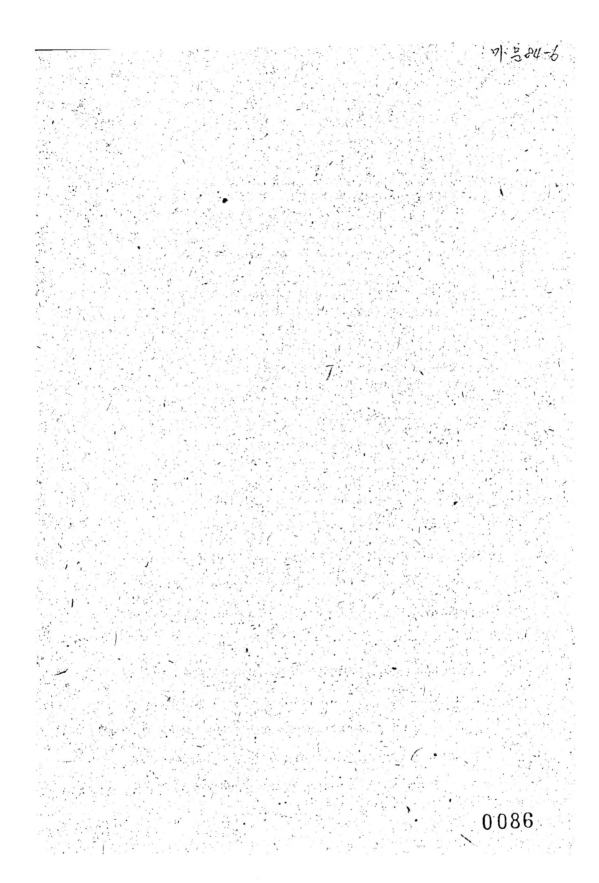

4. If a member of the United Nations forces or of the civilian components or his dependent is, by reason of alteration in his status, no longer entitled to the privileges provided for in the foregoing paragraphs, the United Nations forces authorities shall notify the Korean authorities and shall, if such person be required by the Korean authorities to leave Korea, assure that transportation from Korea will be provided within a reasonable time at no cost to the Korean Government.

ARTICLE III

1. (a) (i) Korea agrees to grant to the Unified Command the use of the facilities and areas necessary to carry out the mission and purposes of the United Nations forces in Korea.

(ii) Agreements as to facilities and areas to be used by the United Nations forces in accordance with this Agreement shall be concluded by the two Parties through the Joint Committee provided for

0087

미: 운84-6

0088

in Article XVII of this Agreement.

(iii) Until such agreement are concluded between the two Parties the United Nations forces shall continue to use such facilities and areas as are being used at the time this Agreement becomes effective.

(b) At the request of either Party, Korea and the Unified Command shall review such arrangements and may agree that such faciliti s and areas shall be returned to Korea or that additional facilities and areas may be provided.

(c) The facilities and areas used by the United Nations forces shall be returned to Korea whenever they are no longer needed for purposes of this Agreement, and the Unified Command agrees to keep the needs for facilities and areas under continual observation with a view toward such return.

(d) When facilities and areas such as target ranges and maneuver grounds are temporarily not being used by the United Nations forces, interim use may be made by Korean authorities and nationals in accordance with the decision made by the Joint Committee provided

0083

for in Article XVII of this Agreement.

2. (a) The Unified Command shall have the rights, power and authority within the facilities and areas which are necessary or appropriate for their establishment, use, operation or defense. The Unified Command shall also have such rights, power and authorities over land, territorial waters and airspace adjacent to, or in the vicinities of such facilities and areas, as are necessary to provide access to such facilities and areas, for their support and defense. In the exercise outside the facilities and areas of the rights, power and authority granted in this Article there should be, as the occasion requires, consultation between the two Parties through the Joint Committee.

(b) The Unified Command agrees that the above mentioned rights, power and authority will not be exercised in such a manner as to interfere unnecessarily with navigation, aviation, communication, or land travel to, of from or within the territories of Korea. All questions relating to frequencies, power and like matters used by apparatus employed by the United Nations forces designed to emit electric radiation shall be settled by

0091

미.북84-6

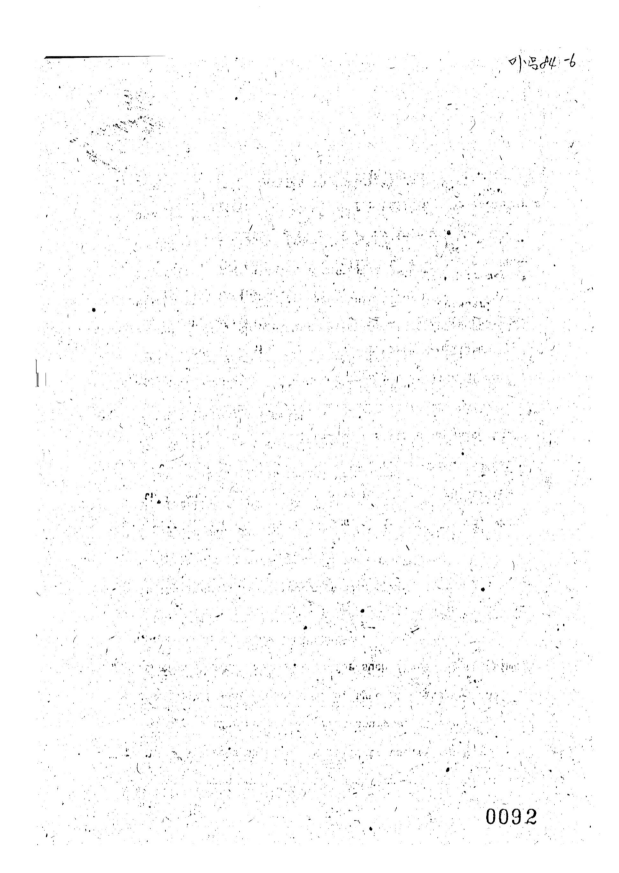

0092

mutual arrangement. Pending such arrangement, the United Nations forces shall be entitled to use, without radiation interference from Korean sources, electronic devices of such power, design, type of emission, and frequencies as are reserved for such forces at the time this Agreement becomes effective.

(c) Operations in the facilities and areas in use by the United Nations forces shall be carried on with due regard for the public safety.

3. (a) The Unified Command is not obliged, when it returns facilities and areas to Korea on the expiration of this Agreement or at an earlier date, to restore the facilities and areas to the condition in which they were at the time they become available to the United Nations forces, or to compensate Korea in lieu of such restoration. In case of private property demolished by such use, the Unified Command shall pay sympathetic consideration to its restoration.

(b) Korea is not obliged to make any compensation to the Unified Command for any improvements made in the facilities and areas or for buildings or structures left thereon the expiration of this Agreement or the

미·문84-6

0094

earlier return of the facilities and areas.

4. (a) Vessels and aircraft operated by, for, or under the control of the United Nations forces for official purposes shall be accorded access to any port or airport of Korea free from toll or landing charges.

When cargo or passengers not accorded the exemption of this Agreement are carried on such vessels and aircraft, notification shall be given to the appropriate Korean authorities, and such cargo or passengers shall be entered in accordance with the laws and regulations of Korea.

(b) When the vessels mentioned paragraph 4(a) enter Korean ports, appropriate notification shall, under normal conditions, be made to the proper Korean authorities. Such vessels shall have freedom from compulsory pilotage, but if a pilot is taken pilotage shall be paid for at appropriate rates.

5. (a) All civil and military air traffic control and communications systems shall be coordinated in accordance with the decision made by Joint Committee.

(b) Lights and other aids to navigation of vessels and aircraft placed or established in the

0095

미.584-6

0096

facilities and areas in use by the United Nations forces and in territorial waters adjacent thereto or in the vicinity thereof shall conform to the system in use in Korea. The Korean and the United Nations forces authorities which have established such navigation aids shall notify each other of their positions and characteristics and shall give advance notification before making any changes in them or establishing additional navigation aids.

6. The United Nations forces may use all public utilities and services belonging to the Government of Korea under conditions no less favorable than those applicable to the armed forces of Korea.

7. Korea and the United Nations forces shall cooperate in meteorological services through exchange of meteorological observation, climatological information and seismographic data.

ARTICLE IV

1. Subject to the provisions of this Article,

(a) the United Nations forces authorities shall have the right to exercise within Korea all cri-

0097

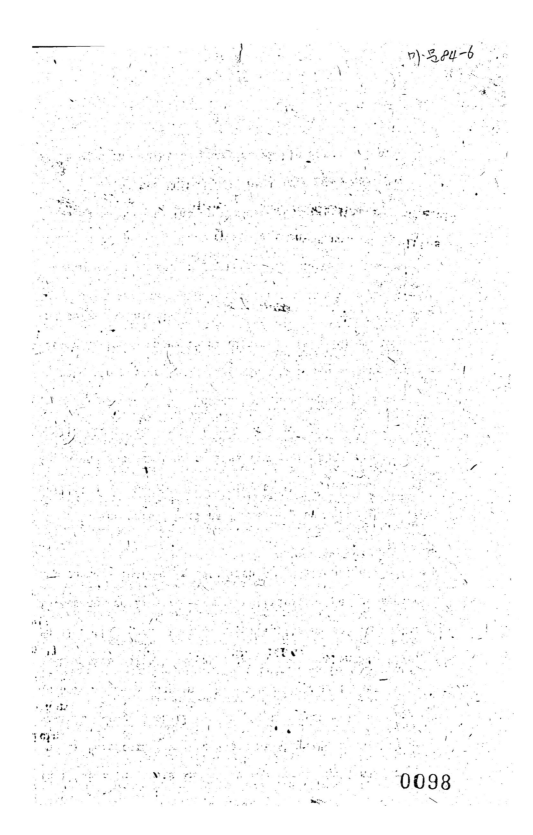

minal and disciplinary jurisdiction conferred on them by the law of the United Nations forces over all persons subject to the military law of the United Nations forces

(b) the authorities of Korea shall have jurisdiction over the members of the United Nations forces or civilian component and their dependents with respect to offences committed within the territory of Korea and punishable by the law of Korea.

2. (a) The United Nations forces authorities shall have the right to exercise exclusive jurisdiction over persons subject to the military law of the United Nations forces with respect to offences, including offences relating to its security, punishable by the law of the United Nations forces, but not by the law of Korea.

(b) The authorities of Korea shall have the right to exercise exclusive jurisdiction over members of the United Nations forces or civilian component and their dependents with respect to offences, including offences relating to the security of Korea, punishable by its law but not by the law of the United Nations forces.

(c) For the purposes of this paragraph and

0100

of paragraph 3 of this Article a security offence against a State shall include,

(i) treason against the State;

(ii) sabotage, espionage or violation of any law relating to official secrets of that State, or secrets relating to the national defense of that State.

3. In case where the right to exercise jurisdiction is concurrent the following rules shall apply:

(a) The United Nations authorities shall have the primary right to exercise jurisdiction over a member of the United Nations forces or of a civilian component in relation to

(i) offences solely against the property or security of the United Nations forces or their states, or offences solely against the person or property of another member of the United Nations forces or civilian component of of a dependent;

(ii) offences arising out of any act or omission done in the execution of

0101

미문244-6

0102

official duty.

(b) In the case of any other offence the authoritées of Korea shall have the primary right to exercise jurisdiction.

(c) If the Party having the primary right decide not to exercise jurisdiction, it shall notify the authorities of the other Party as soon as practicable. The authorities of the Party having the primary right shall give sympathetic consideration to a request from the authorities of the other Party for a waiver of its right in cases where that other Party considers such waiver to be of particular importance.

4. The foregoing provisions of this Article shall not imply any right for the United Nations forces authorities to exercise jurisdiction over persons who are nationals of rodinarily resident in Korea, unless they are members of the United Nations forces.

5. (a) The authorities of Korea and the United Nations forces authorities shall assist each other in the arrest of members of the United Nations forces or

0103

미문84-6

0104

civilian component or their dependents in the territory of Korea and in handing them over to the authority which is to exercise jurisdiction in accordance with the above provisions.

(b) The authorities of Korea shall notify promptly the United Nations forces authorities of the arrest of any member of the United Nations forces or civilian component or a dependent.

(c) The custody of an accused member of the United Nations forces or civilian component over whom Korea is to exercise jurisdiction shall, if he is in the hands of the United Nations forces remain with the United Nations forces until he is charged by Korea.

6. (a) The authorities of Korea and the United Nations forces authorities shall assist each other in the carrying out of all encessary investigations into offences, and in the collection and production of evidence, including seizure and, in proper cases, the handing over of objects connected with an offense, The handing over of such objects may, however, be made subject to their return within the time specified by

미무84-6

0106

the authorities delivering them.

(b) The authorities of Korea and the United Nations forces shall notify each other of the disposition of all cases in which there are concurrent rights to exercise jurisdiction.

7. (a) A death sentense shall not be carried out in Korea by the United Nations forces authorities if the legislation of Korea does not provide for such punishment in a similar case.

(b) The authorities of Korea shall have sympathetic consideration to a request from the United Nations forces authorities for assistance in carrying out a sentense of imprisonment pronounced by the United Nations forces authorities under the provisions of this Article within the territory of Korea.

8. Where an accused has been tried in accordance with provisions of this Article either by the authorities of Korea or the United Nations forces authorities and has been acquitted, or has been convicted and is serving or has served, or his sentence has been pardoned,

0107

0108

he may not be tried again for the same offence within the territory by the authorities of the other Party. However, nothing in this paragraph shall prevent the United Nations forces authorities from trying a member of its armed forces for any violation of rules of discipline arising from an act or omission which constituted an offence for which he was tried by the authorities of Korea.

9. Whenever a member of the United Nations forces or civilian component or a dependent is prosecuted under the jurisdiction of Korea he shall be entitled:

(a) to a prompt and speedy trial;

(b) to be informed, in advance of trial, of specific charge made against him;

(c) to be confromted with the witnesses against him;

(d) to have compulsory process for obtaining witnesses in his favor, if they are within the jurisdiction of Korea.

(e) to have legal representation of his own choice for his defense or to have free

0109

미:문84-6
0110

or assisted legal representation under the conditions prevailing for the time being in Korea;

(f) if he considers it necessary, to have the services of a competent interpreter; and

(g) to communicate with a representative of the United Nations forces and, when the rules of the court permit, to have such a representative present at his trial.

10. (a) Regularly constituted military units or formations of the United Nations forces shall have the right to police any facilities or areas which they use under Article III of this Agreement. The military police of such forces may take all appropriate measures to ensure the maintenance of order and security within such facilities and areas.

(b) Outside these facilities and areas, such military police shall be employed only subject to arrangements with the authorities of Korea and in liaison

0111

0112

with those authorities, and in so far as such employment is necessary to maintain discipline and order among the members of the United Nations forces.

ARTICLE V

1. Each Party waives all its claims against the other Party for damage to any property in Korea owned by it and used by its land, sea or air armed services, if such damage

(i) was caused by a member or an employee of the armed services of the other Party, in the execution of his official duties; or

(ii) arose from the use of any vehicle, vessel or aircraft owned by theother Party and used by its armed services, provided either that the vehicle, vessel or aircraft causing the damage was being used in the execution of its official duty or that the damage

0113

마84-6

0114

was caused to property being so used.

Claims for maritime salvage by one Party against the other Party shall be waived, provided that the vessel or cargo salved was owned by the former, and being used by its armed services in the execution of their official duties.

2. (a) In the case of damage caused or arising as stated in paragraph 1 to other property in Korea owned by either Party the issue of the liability of the other Party shall be determined and the amount of damage shall be assessed, unless the two Parties agree otherwise, by the Joint Committee to be established under Artucle XVII of this Agreement.

(b) Payment of the amount of any compensation decided by the Joint Committee shall be made in Korean currency.

3. Each Party waives all its claims against the otherParty for injury or death suffered in Korea by a member or an employee of its armed forces, while such member or employee was engaged in the execution of his

0115

미-584-6
0116

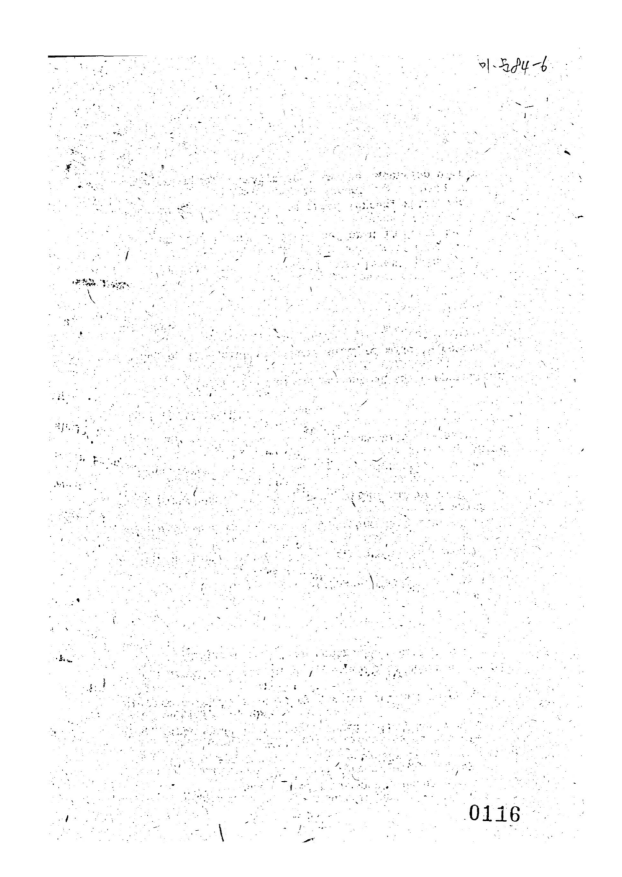

official duties in case where such injury or death was caused by a member of the armed forces, or an employee of the other Party acting in the execution of his official duties.

4. Claims (other than contractual claims and those to which paragraph 5 or 6 of this Article shall apply) arising out of acts or omissions of members of or employees of the United Nations forces or civilian component done in the execution of official duty, or out of any other act, omission or occurrence for which the United Nations forces or civilian component is legally responsible, and causing damage in Korea to third Parties, shall be dealt with by Korea in accordance with the follwoing provisions:

(a) Claims shall be filed, considered and settled or adjudicated in accordance with the laws and regulations of Korea with respect to claims arising from the activities of its own armed forces.

(b) Korea may settle any such claims, and payment of the amount agreed upon or

0117

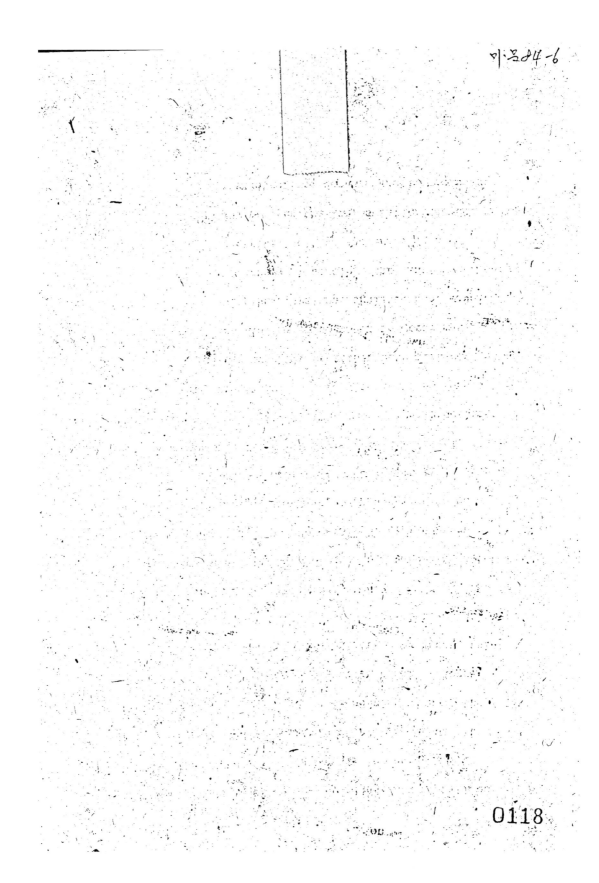

미·844-6
0118

determined by adjudication shall be made by Korea in its currency.

(c) Such payment, whether made pursuant to a settlement or to adjudication of the case by a competent tribunal of Korea, or the final adjudication by such a tribunal denying payment, shall be binding and conclusive.

(d) The cost incurred in the course of settling or adjudicating claims pursuant to the preceeding subparagraph to be agreed by the two Parties shall be shared on terms.

(e) Every claim paid by Korea shall be communicated to the United Nations forces periodically, together with full particulars and request for reimbursement. Such reimbursement shall be made within the shortest possible time in the currency of Korea.

(f) A member of the United Nations forces or civilian component shall not be subject

0119

to any preceeding for the enforcement of any judgement given against him in Korea in a matter arising from the execution of his official duties.

5. Claims against members of the United Nations forces or civilian component arising out of tortious acts or omissions in Korea not done in the execution of official duty shall be dealt with in the following manner:

(a) The Korean authorities shall consider the claim and assess compensation to the claimant in a fair and just manner, taking into account all the circumstances of the case, including the conduct of the injured person, and shall prepare a report on the matter.

(b) The report shall be delivered to the United Nations forces authorities, who shall then decide without delay whether they will offer an *ex gratia* payment, and if so, of what amount.

0121

미문P4-6
0122

(c) If an offer of ex gratia payment is made, and accepted by the claimant in full satisfaction of his claim, the United Nations forces authorities shall make the payment themselves and inform the Korean authorities of their decision and of the sum paid.

(d) Nothing in this paragraph shall affect the jurisdiction of the courts of Korea to entertain an action against a member of the United Nations forces or of a civilian component unless and until there has been payment in full satisfaction of the claim.

6. Claims arising out of the unauthorized use of any vehicle of the United Nations forces shall be dealt with in accordance with paragraph 5 of this Article, except in so far as the armed forces or civilian component is legally responsible.

7. Each Party shall have the primary right, in the execution of the foregoing paragraphs, to determine

0123

미·문84-6
0124

whether its personnel were engaged in the execution of official duty. Such determination shall be made as soon as possible after the arising of theclaim concerned. When the other Party disagrees with the results of such determination, that Party may bring the matter before the Joint Committee for consultation under the provisions of Article XVI.

8. The Unified Command shall not claim immunity from the jurisdiction of the courts of Korea for members of its armed forces or civilian component in respect of the civil jurisdiction of the courts of Korea except to the extent provided in paragraph 4 (f) of this Article.

9. The authorities of Korea and the United Nations forces authorities shall cooperate in the procurement of evidence for a fair hearing and disposal of claims in regard to which the two Parties are concerned.

10. In case any private movable property, excluding that in use by the United Nations forces, which is subject to compulsory execution under Korean law, is

0125

0126

within the facilities and areas in use by the United Nations forces, the United Nations forces authorities shall upon the request of Korean courts, possess and turn over such property to the Korean authorities.

ARTICLE VI

1. Members of the United Nations forces or civilian component and their dependents may purchase locally goods necessary for their own consumption, and such services as they need, under the same conditions as the nationals of Korea.

2. Goods and services which are required and can be procured from local sources for the subsistance of the United Nations forces or civilian component shall be procured, in conformation to the United Nations policy to aid Korean economy, in a manner most likely to help maintain Korean economical stability and least to adversely affect it, and in coordination with and, when desirable, through or with the assistance of the competent authorities of Korea.

0127

미.584-6
0128

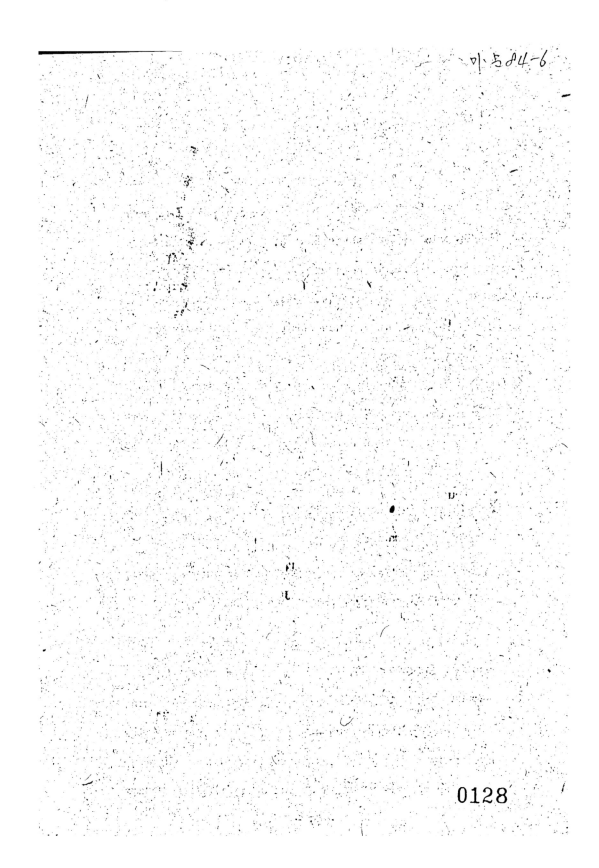

3. Local civilian labor requirements of the United Nations forces or civilian component shall be satisfied with the assistance of the Korean authorities. Care should be constantly taken, however, not to unnecessarily strain Korean manpower so that equally or more important projects may not suffer from lack of hands.

4. Except as may otherwise mutually be agreed, the conditions of employment and work, such as those relating wages, supplementary payments, and conditions for the protection of workers, shall be those laid down by the legislation of Korea.

5. The United Nations forces shall refrain from employing foreign laborers in the territory of Korea as well as its territorial waters with a view to not compromising the employment of Korean laborers.

ARTICLE VII

1. The United Nations forces shall not be subject to taxes or similar charges on property held, used or transferred by such forces in Korea.

0120

미·군84-6

0130

2. Members of the United Nations forces, the civilian component, and their dependents shall not be liable to pay any Korean taxes to the Korean Government or to any other taxing agency in Korea on income received as a result of their service with or employment by the United Nations forces, or by the organizations provided for in Article IX.

3. Nothing in this Article shall prevent taxation members of the United Nations forces or civilian component or their dependents with respect to any income derived from sources other than those provided for in paragraph 2 of this Article.

4. Members of the United Nations forces, the civilian component and their dependents shall be exempt from taxation with respect to any movable property, the presence of which in Korea is due solely to their temporary presence in Korea, provided that such exemption shall not apply to property held for the purpose of investment or the conduct of business in Korea.

0131

아 문84-6

0132

ARTICLE VIII

1. Save as provided to the contrary in this Agreement, members of the United Nations forces, the civilian component, and their dependents shall be subject to the laws and regulations administered by the customs authorities of Korea.

2. The United Nations forces or the organizations provided for in Article IX may import free of duty all materials, supplies and equipment, exclusively for the official use of the United Nations forces or for the use of the members of the United Nations forces, the civilian component, and their dependents. The duty free importation shall be verified by a certificate issued by the United Nations forces authorities in a form agreed between Korea and the United Nations forces.

3. Property consigned to and for the personal use of members of the United Nations forces, the civilian component, and their dependents, shall be subject to customs duties, except that no duties shall be paid with respect to:

0133

미.무 84-6

0134

(a) Furniture, household goods and other personal effects for their private use imported by the members of the United Nations forces, civilian component and their dependents at the time of their first arrival in Korea;

(b) Reasonable quantities of clothing and household goods of a type which would ordinarily be pruchased in their home states for everyday use for the private use of members of the United Nations forces, civilian component, and their dependents, which are mailed into Korea through the United Nations forces military post offices.

4. Official documents under official seal and mail in the United Nations forces postal channels shall not be subject to customs inspection.

5. Goods which have imported duty-free under paragraph 2 and 3 above:

0135

미·문84-6
0136

(a) may be re-exported freely, provided that, in the case of goods imported under paragraph 2, a certificate is issued by the United Nations forces authorities in a form agreed between Korea and the United Nations forces;

(b) shall not normally be disposed of in Korea by way of either sale or gift. However, in particular cases such disposal may be authorized on conditions agreed between the authorities of Korea and the United Nations forces.

6. Exportation and re-importation goods purchased in Korea shall be subject to the regulations in force in Korea. Such goods shall be regarded exported when deposited in a warehouse and deemed imported when removed from the warehouse.

7. In paragraph 2, 3 and 5 of this Article, "duty" means customs duties and all other duties and taxes payable on importation or exportation, as the case may be,

0137

미문84-6

0138

except dues and taxes which are no more than charges for services rendered.

8. (a) The customs authorities of Korea shall have the right, when desirable, in cooperation with the authorities of the United Nations forces to search members of the United Nations forces or civilian component and their dependents and examine their luggage and vehicles, and to seize articles pursuant to the laws and regulations administered by the customs authorities of Korea.

(b) In order to prevent offences against customs and fiscal laws and regulations, the authorities of Korea and of the United Nations forces shall assist each other in the conduct of inquiries and the collection of evidence.

(c) The authorities of the United Nations forces shall render all assistance within their power to ensure that articles liable to seizure by, or on behalf of, the customs or fiscal authorities of Korea are handed to those authorities.

(d) The authorities of the United Nations

0139

0140

forces shall render all assistance within their power to ensure the payment of duties, taxes and penalties payable by members of the United Nations forces or civilian component or their dependents.

ARTICLE IX

1. (a) Navy exchange, post exchange, messes, social clubs, theaters, newspapers and other non-appropriated funds organizations authorized and regulated by the United Nations forces authorities may be established in the facilities and areas in use by the United Nations forces for the use of members of such forces, the civilian component, and their dependents. Except as otherwise provided in this Agreement, such organizations shall not be subject to Korean regulations, license, fees, taxes or similar controls.

(b) When a newspaper authorized and regulated by the United Nations forces authorities is sold to the general public, it shall be subject to Korean regulations, license, fees, taxes or similar controls so far as such circulation is concerned.

0141

0142

2. No Korean tax shall be imposed on sales of merchandise and services by such organizations, except as provided in paragraph 1 (b) of this Article, but purchases within Korea of merchandise and supplies by such organizations shall be subject to Korean taxes.

3. Except as such disposal may be authorized by the Korean and the United Nations forces authorities in accordance with mutually agreed conditions, goods which are sold by such organizations shall not be disposed of in Korea to persons not authorized to make purchases from such organizations.

4. The organizations referred to in this Article shall provide such information to the Korean authorities as is required by Korean legislations.

ARTICLE X

The Unified Command shall have the right to establish and operate, within the facilities and areas in use by the United Nations forces, the United Nations forces military post offices for the use of members

0143

기.문84-6

0144

of the United Nations forces, the civilian component and their dependents, for the transmission of mail between the United Nations forces military post offices in Korea and between such military post offices and their home States post offices.

ARTICLE XI

Korea shall accept as valid, without a driving test or fee, the driving permit or license or military driving permit issued by the States sending the United Nations forces under the Unified Command to a member of the United Nations forces, the civilian component, and their dependents.

ARTICLE XII

1. Members of the United Nations forces shall normally wear uniform. Subject to any arrangement to the contrary between the authorities of Korea and the United Nations forces, the wearing of civilian dress shall be on the same conditions as for members of the

미·584-6

0146

armed forces of Korea.

2. Official vehicles of the United Nations forces and the civilian component shall carry a distinctive nationality mark and individual markings which will readily identify them.

3. Privately owned vehicles of members of the United Nations forces, the civilian component, and their dependents shall carry Korean number plates to be acquired under the same conditions as those applicable to Korean nationals.

ARTICLE XIII

1. Members of the United Nations forces or civilian component may possess and carry arms, on condition that they are authorized to do so by their orders. The authorities of the United Nations forces shall give sympathetic consideration to request from Korea concerning this matter.

2. Dependents of members of the United Nations

마문84-6

0148

forces or of civilian component may possess and carry arms in accordance with the laws and regulations of Korea.

ARTICLE XIV

Members of the United Nations forces, the civilian component, and their dependents shall respect the law of Korea and abstain from any activities inconsistant with the spirit of this Agreement, and, in particular, shall not engage in any political activity in Korea.

ARTICLE XV

In the event of hostilities, or imminently threatened hostilities, in Korea, the Governments of Korea and the Unified Command shall immediately consult together with a view to agreeing on such modifications as they may consider desirable regarding the application of this Agreement.

0143

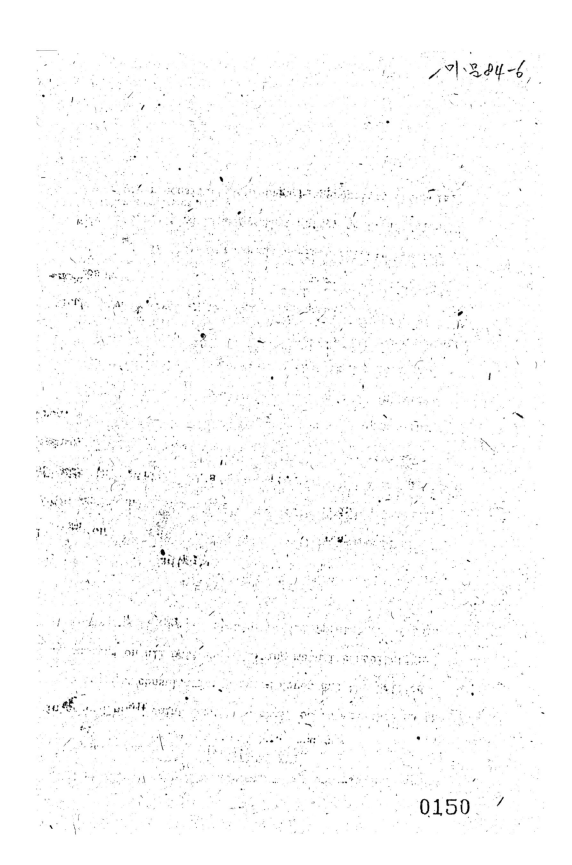

ARTICLE XVI

1. A Joint Committee shall be established as the means for consultation between Korea and the Unified Command on all matters requiring mutual consultation regarding the implementation or interpretation of this Agreement.

2. The Joint Committee shall be composed of a representative of Korea and of the Unified Command, each of whom shall have one or more deputies and a staff. The Joint Committee shall determine its own procedures, and arrange for such military organs and administrative services as may be required. The Joint Committee shall be so organized that it may meet immediately at any time at the request of the representative of either Korea or the Unified Command.

3. If the Joint Committee is unable to resolve any matter, it shall refer that matter to the Parties for further consideration through appropriate channels.

0151

0152

ARTICLE XVII

This Agreement shall come into force on the date of signature by the representatives of Korea and of the Unified Command.

ARTICLE XVIII

Either Party may at any time request the revision of any Article of this Agreement. The request shall be addressed to the Joint Committee.

ARTICLE XIX

This Agreement and agreed revisions thereof, shall remain in force while the United Nations forces stay in Korea.

This Agreement shall be suspended upon the withdrawal of the United Nations forces from Korea, and shall resume its force automatically whenever such forces

0153

미문84-6
0154

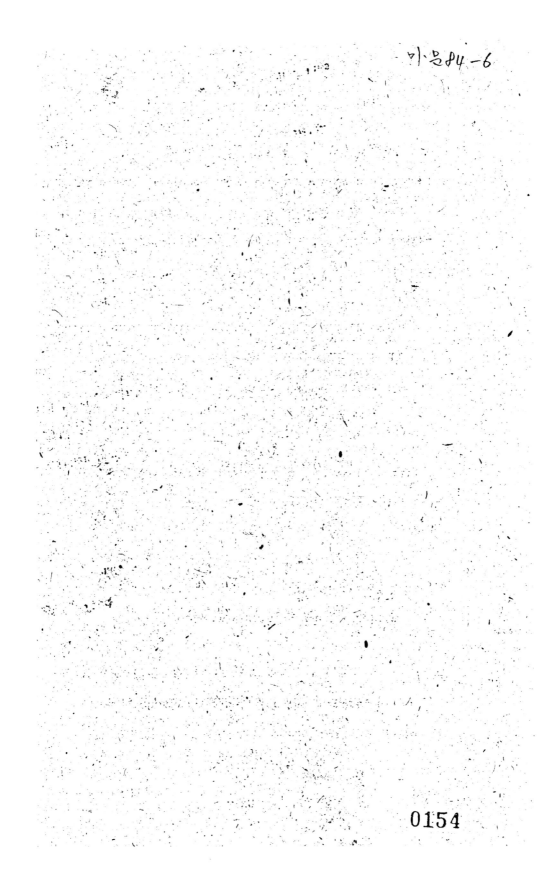

return to Korea.

IN WITNESS WHEREOF the representatives of the two Parties duly authorized for the purpose, have signed this Agreement.

DONE in Seoul, in duplicate, in the Korean and English languages, both equally authentic, this the day of 1955.

For the Government of the Republic of Korea:

For the Government of the United States of America acting as the Unified Command:

0155

미문 84-6(42)

0156

7. United States Charge d'Affaires' reply of May 9, 1955 to the Foreign Minister's letter of April 28, 1955.

American Embassy,
Seoul, Korea,
May 9, 1955.

My dear Mr. Minister:

I have the honor to acknowledge the receipt of your letter of April 28, 1955, enclosing a Draft of an Administrative Agreement between the Republic of Korea and the Unified Command regarding the Status of the United Nations Forces.

I note that you request that negotiations be commenced between representatives of the Governments of the United States and of the Republic of Korea looking toward the completion of an agreement.

I have transmitted a copy of the Ministry's Draft to the Department of State and have asked for the Department's instructions. I shall be pleased to advise you as soon as these are received and shall look forward to a happy outcome of our negotiations.

0157

Accept, Mr. Minister, the assurances of my highest consideration.

/s/

His Excellency
Pyun, Yung-tai
Minister of Foreign Affairs,
Republic of Korea.

0159

미문84-7(2)
0160

8. General Lemnitzer's letter of July 26, 1955 to the Foreign Minister.

26 July 1955

Dear Minister Pyun:

Thank you very much for your letter of 13 June 1955, in which you acknowledge receipt of General Taylor's letter of 14 May 1955, with the inclosures pertaining to customs functions of the Republic of Korea.

I have noted the desire of the Korean Government to commence negotiations with the Government of the United States for a Status of Forces Agreement between the Korean Government and the Unified Command. This matter is presently under study by the Department of my government in Washington.

Current thinking on this matter is that it would be preferable that negotiations now in progress or pending be completed before the initiation of negotiations for an agreement of the type in question. Ambassador Lacy advises me that a proposed treaty of

0161

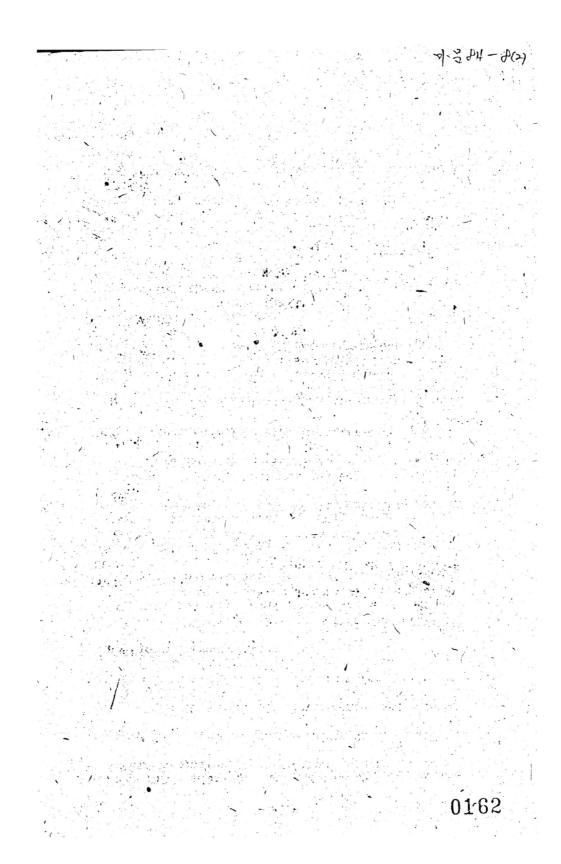

friendship, commerce and navigation between our respective governments is under consideration, as well as an agreement guaranteeing investments, and that he is anxious to complete these matters before taking up any other major negotiations.

I am sure you are also aware that the Unfied Command cannot participate in a negotiation of any Status of Forces Agreement without the prior consent of our allies within the United Nations Command. It is anticipated that the task of obtaining this consent will be difficult and time consuming.

Sincerely,

/s/
L.L. LEMNITZER
General, United States Army
Commander-in-Chief

His Excellency Pyun Yung-Tai
Minister for Foreign Affairs of
The Republic of Korea

0163

미동84-8(2)

0164

9. Foreign Minister's reply of July 28, 1955 to the General Lemnitzer's letter of July 26, 1955.

July 28, 1955

My dear General,

Let me acknowledge with thanks the receipt of your good letter of July 26, 1955 regarding the negotiation of an administrative agreement between the Unified Command and this Government. An agreement of this nature has been long due and your note of concurrence in the wish of concluding one is most welcome and heartening.

Since the Unfied Command is reposed in the American hands and since the American forces form the predominant components of the United Nations forces, we need not envisage real difficulties in securing consent of other allies in the matter.

As regards the treaty of friendship, commerce and navigation, it is near completion, awaiting to be finalized very soon, and the agreement guaranteeing investments, already in complete draft form, will not

0165

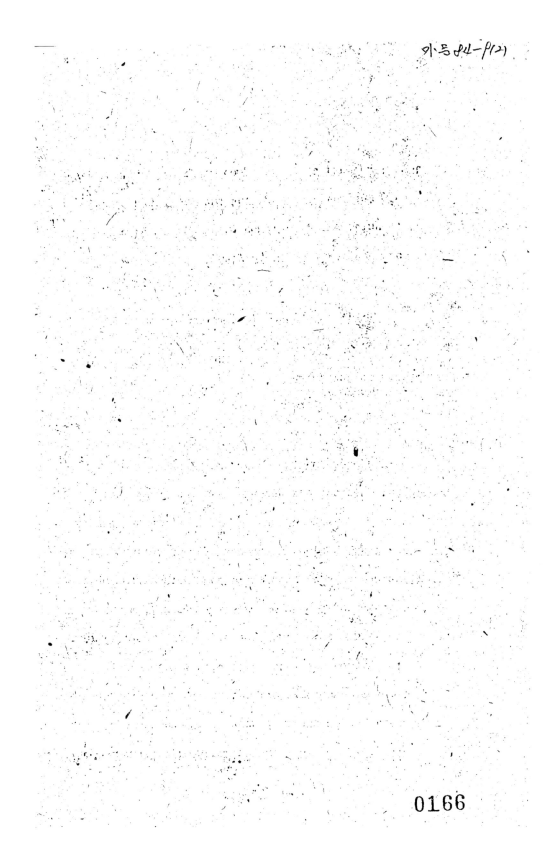

consume such time in negotiation.

This Government is very desirous of starting the negotiation for an administrative agreement immediately after the two aforementioned treates are concluded. Our allies, too, fully aware of the need of such an agreement, will not, I am sure, make difficulties about starting preliminary negotiation for it simultaneously with the Unified Command seeking to obtain their consent as to the matter.

Thanking you once again for the long awaited offer,

Yours sincerely,

/s/
Y. T. Pyun
Minister of Foreign Affairs

Genetal L. L. LEMNITZER
Commander-in-Chief
United Nations Command

0167

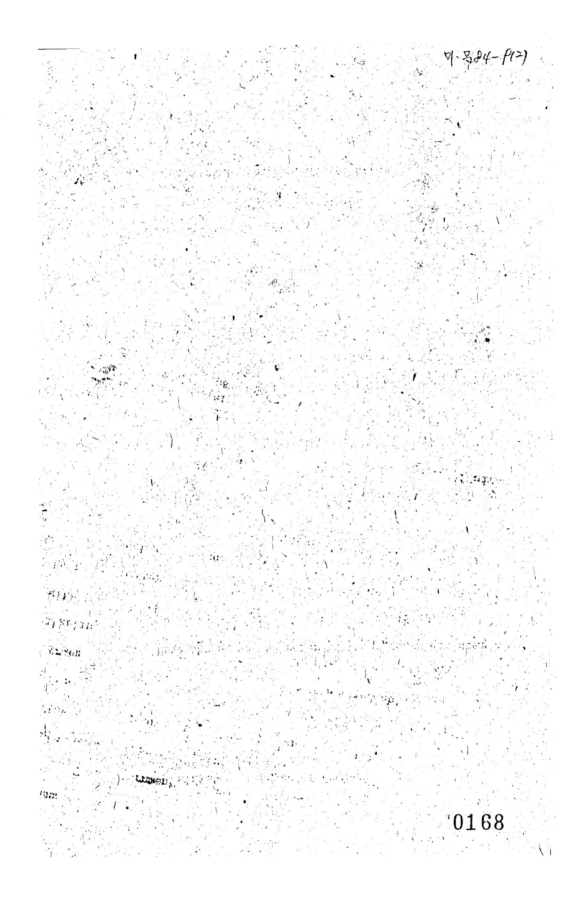

10. Foreign Minister's letter of January 5, 1957 to the United States Ambassador.

January 5, 1957

Excellency:

I have the honour to refer to the Foreign Minister's note addressed to Mr. Carl W. Strom, Charge d'Affaire ad interim of the Embassy of the United States of America in Korea dated April 28, 1955 enclosing a draft of an Administrative Agreement between the Republic of Korea and the Unified Command for establishment of the Status of the United Nations Forces in Korea.

In the afore-said note, the Minister informed the Government of the United States of America of the desire of the Korean Government to commence negotiations with the United States Government for the said Status of Forces Agreement which will also define the former's

His Excellency
The right honourable
Walter C. Dowling
Ambassador of the United States of
America to the Republic of Korea
Seoul, Korea

0169

미·보84-10(A)

0170

customs functions as referred to in my letter of December 2, 1954.

To this proposal, however, no acceptance has been given as yet, although the American Charge d'Affairs notified in his replying note of May 9, 1955, that upon obtaining his Government's view on the said request, he would communicate with the Minister.

I hereby wish again to propose, on behalf of my Government, that negotiation be commenced at an earliest possible date between the representatives of the Korean Government and the United States Government. In connection with this re-proposal, I would like further to refer to the note of July 26, 1955 addressed to the Foreign Minister by General Lemnitzer advising on this matter.

General Lemnitzer expressed his views on the possibility of negotiating the said agreement in the above note to the effect that the United States Government envisages difficulties in commencing immediately negotiations for a proposed agreement for the following two reasons:

The one reason was that it would be preferable to

미822-10

0172

the American Government that negotiations for a proposed treaty of Friendship, Commerce and Navigation between the two countries as well as an agreement guaranteeing investments be completed before the initiation of negotiation for an agreement in question. The other was that the Unified Command cannot participate in negotiation of such agreement without the prior consent of allies within the Unified Command and it is anticipated that the task of obtaining such consent will be difficult.

Attention, however, is paid to the fact that the points indicated above constitute no longer difficulties about negotiating the said agreement under the present circumstances.

The Treaty of Friendship, Commerce and Navigation has been already signed and is now waiting to be formally ratified. As regards the agreement guaranteeing investments, discussions have been completed on provisions of its draft and now the work of finalizing it remains only. On the other hand, since allies within the Unified Command have been decreased in number into twelve nations and since the American forces form the predominant components of the United Nations Forces, there exist no

0173

마 8844-10
0174

difficulties, it is believed, in securing consent of other allies as to the matter.

And thus, even in case the consent of the other allies has not been obtained as yet, it is, therefore, proposed that negotiations be started first between both representatives of the Korean Government and the United States Government and that negotiations with other allies shall be carried on seperately in accordance with terms to be agreed upon between Korea and the United States of America. It is sincrely requested that the concurrence of the United States Government be given to the wish of the Korean Government to commence negotiations for the agreement proposed.

Please accept, Excellency, the renewed assurances of my highest consideration.

/s/
Chung W. Cho
Minister
of Foreign Affairs

0175

미,등84-10(4)

0176

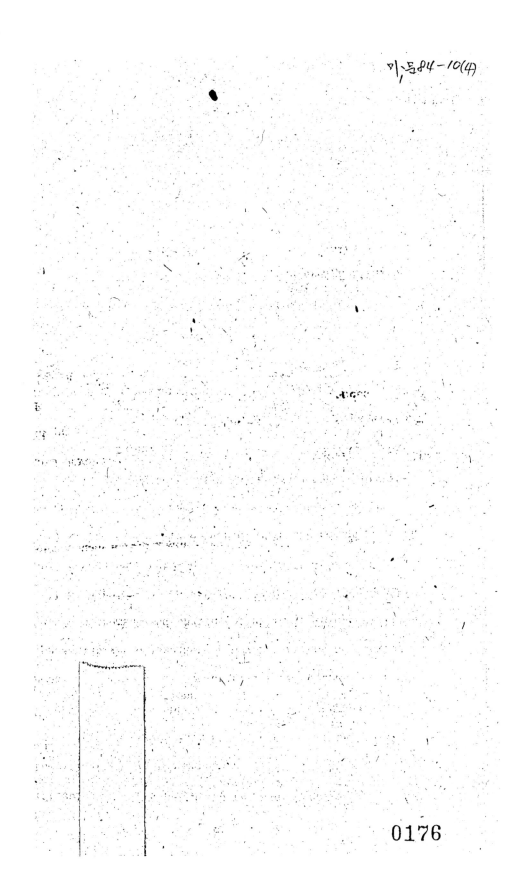

11. United States Ambassador's reply of January 15, 1957 to the Foreign Minister's letter of January 5, 1957.

American Embassy,
Seoul, Korea,
January 15, 1957.

Excellency:

I have the honor to acknowledge the receipt of your note of January 5, 1957, proposing that negotiations be commenced at the earliest possible date between the representatives of the Republic of Korea and of the Unified Command for Establishment of the Status of the United Nations Forces in Korea as proposed by the Government of the Republic of Korea in a draft transmitted on April 28, 1955.

I have transmitted a copy of your note to my Government, and have requested its instructions. I shall look forward to further consultation with you as soon as these instructions have been received.

Please accept, Excellency, the renewed assurances of my highest consideration.

/s/

0177

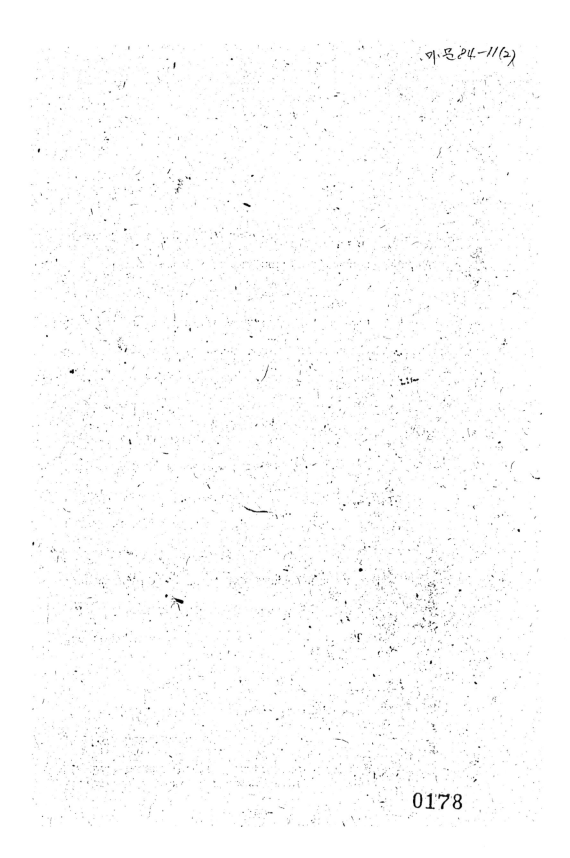

미.문 84-11(2)
0178

His Excellency

Cho Chung-hwan,

Minister for Foreign Affairs,

Republic of Korea,

Seoul.

0179

미·무 84-11(2)

0180

12. Memorandum of February 4, 1957 from First Secretary Han You-Dong to Minister Han Pyo-Ook.

February 4, 1957

MEMORANDUM: TO Minister Han

SUBJECT: Administrative Agreement

FROM: First Secretary Han

I had a conference this morning on the above subject with Mr. David Nes, Chief of Korea Desk of the State Department. As you know, our Government wants to commence negotiations on this subject and has instructed this Embassy to expedite the matter at this end.

Mr. Nes said that only a few days ago the State Department received a dispatch from its Embassy in Seoul enclosing the latest letter (dated January 5, 1957) from Foreign Minister Cho to Ambassaodr Dowling. He said that inasmuch as this problem involves

0181

미일84-12(4)

0182

the Defense Department and legal authorities, the State Department cannot decide alone what to do and will have to have interdepartmental conferences before a decision can be reached. He estimated that four to six weeks would be required for this purpose. He promised to work on it actively and said he will let us know as soon as his government decides what to do. At the same time, he said, a detailed reply will be sent to Foreign Minister Cho through the Embassy in Seoul.

Commenting on the difficulty of starting negotiations on this matter, Mr. Nes said that legally Korea is still in a state of war and that it would be difficult for the United States to negotiate an administrative agreement such as that exists with NATO countries or with Japan. He mentioned that in the Treaty with NATO countries, there is a provision that provides for instant termination of the Treaty in

0183

case of a war.

I said that this matter of Administ-ative Agreement was first taken up by our government in April, 1955, at which time we presented to the American Embassy in Seoul a draft of the Agreement for its study. I said that although there were several ex-changes of communications with the Embassy in Seoul and also with Gen. Lemnitzer after that, no definite reply has yet been given by the U.S. Government. I said that accord-ing to General Lemnitzer's letter to our Foreign Minister dated July 26, 1955, there were two reasons why negotiations could not be started. First, the U.S. government pre-ferred to start negotiations after the Treaty of Friendship, Commerce and Navigation had been signed. Second, the United States had to get prior consent of the countries whose forces are in the United Nations Forces. The first reason, I said, no longer exists. As for the second reason, I said it should

0185

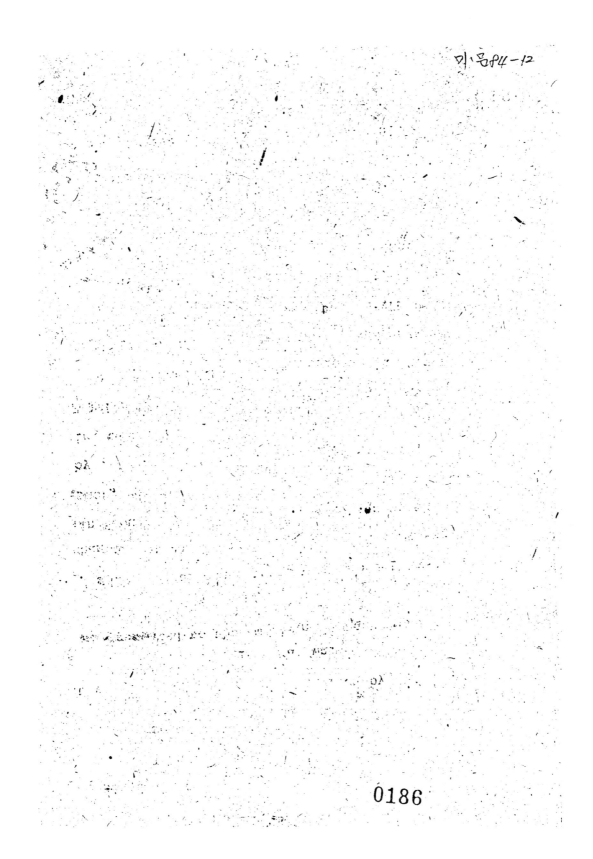

not be too difficult if our two governments started negotiations first and then arrived at a conclusion as to the draft of the Agreement, and then got the Allies concerned to agree to it or negotiate on it. Whatever we do, I said, something should be done to get the ball rolling.

Mr. Nes replied that although Gen. Lemnitzer gave those two reasons, he, or rather, the State Department does not think that they constituted the major difficulties. The State Department believes, he said, that the major difficulty lies in that Korea is still legally in a state of war. Anyway, he said, no definite answer could be given unless some conclusions were reached at inter-departmental conferences, after which both our Foreign Minister and this Embassy would be notified in detail as to what the American position is on the matter.

0187

미도84-12(4)
0188

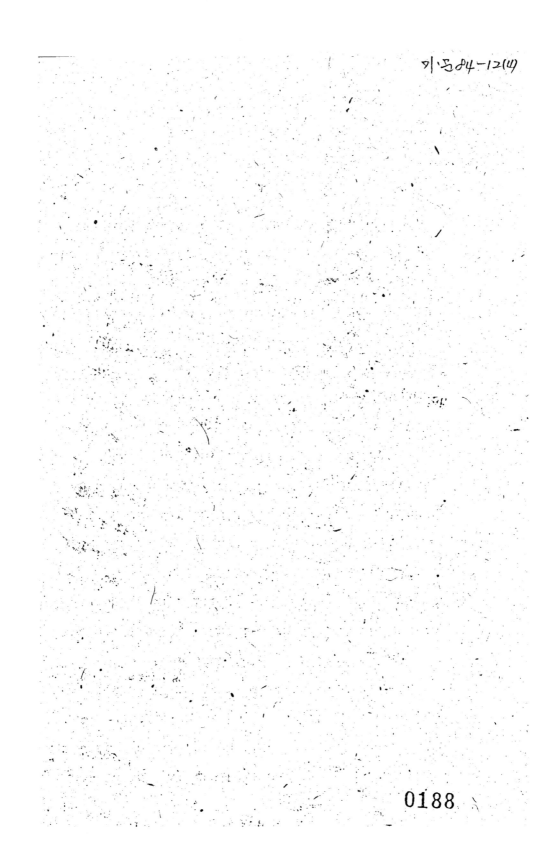

13. Foreign Minister's letter of June 29, 1957 to the United States Ambassador.

June 29, 1957

My dear Mr. Ambassador:

I have the honor to remind your Government, as I have orally mentioned to you on several occasions, that the conclusion of an Administrative Agreement defining and setting forth in detail the status of United States troops stationed in Korea is still pending.

On April 28, 1955, our draft proposal of an Administrative Agreement between this Government and the Unified Command, to establish the status of United Natioons forces in Korea, was addressed to your Embassy. On November 1, 1956, it was proposed that a separate agreement be negotiated between representatives of this Government and the United States Government, in case of dif-

His Excellency
Ambassador Walter Dowling,
American Embassy,
Seoul.

0189

미·문84-13(3)

0190

ficulty in obtaining early consent of the other Allied Governments.

In the absense of such administrative agreement, a temporary agreement was made through the exchange of Notes at Taejon, on July 12, 1950, concerning the exclusive jurisdiction by court-martial of the United States over members of the United States Military Establishment in Korea. This agreement, which is still in force, was improvised to meet an evergency situation and is not considered sufficient to meet effectively all the complex and complicated problems arising from the presence of United States troops in Korea.

This Government is strongly convinced that the early conclusion of a formal and detailed agreement on the status of United States troops in Korea would serve to strengthen cordial relations between our people and American military personnel, and would provide great satisfaction to the mutual cause and interest of both countries.

I wish to state again that this Government is most desirous of receiving the concurrence of the United States Government in order to commence negotiations for

미일24-13

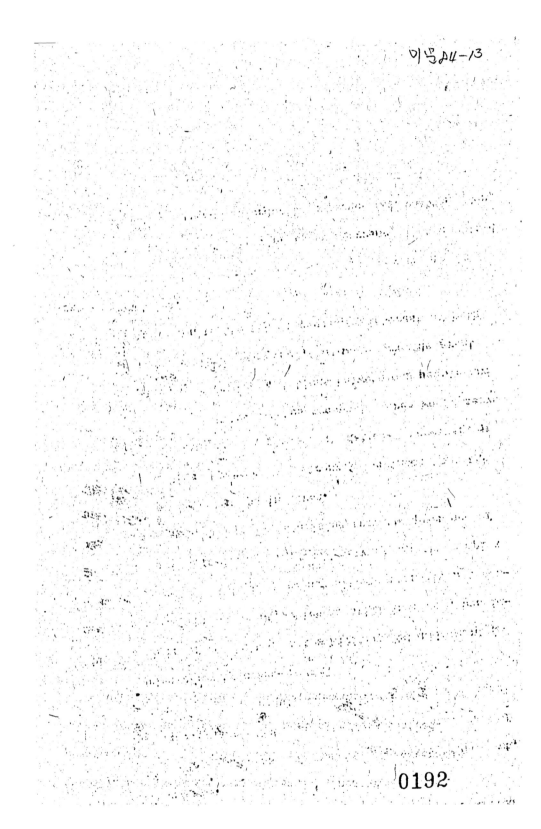

0192

an administrative Agreement along the lines of the proposal of April, 1955. Your Government's earliest favorable consideration of this matter is most sincerely desired.

Accept, Excellency, renewed assurances of my highest consideration.

/s/

Chung W. Cho
Minister.

0193

0194

14. United States Ambassador's reply of July 1, 1957 to the Foreign Minister's letter of June 29, 1957.

American Embassy,
Seoul, Korea,
July 1, 1957

My dear Mr. Minister:

I have the honor to acknowledge receipt of your letter of June 29, 1957, concerning the desire of your Government to negotiate an Administrative Agreement defining the status of United States troops stationed in Korea, and to inform you that the substance of the letter has been cabled to the Department of State.

In this connection I am glad to inform you that your Government's note of January 5, 1957 is currently being given careful consideration in Washimgton. I shall, of course, communicate with you again as soon as I receive pertinent information.

With renewed assurnaces of my highest considerat-ion, I am

Faithfully yours,

/s/ Walter C. Dowling

0195

미.울84-14(2)

0196

His Excellency

Chung W. Cho

Minister of Foreign Affairs,

Republic of Korea.

-0197

미문84-14(2)

0198

15. ROK Government's views of September 10, 1957 handed over to the Under Secretary of State Herter of the United States.

September 10, 1957

SUBJECT: Proposed Agreement on the Status of United Nations or United States Forces in Korea

The Government of the Republic of Korea, keenly desiring to conclude an agreement which would define the status of the United Nations armed forces in Korea, with the Government of the United States of America acting for the Unified Command, in accordance with "The Resolution on the Settlement of the Unified Command" of the Security Council of the United Nations of July 7, 1950, initially proposed to the Government of the United States of American through the Foreign Minister's note of April 28, 1955, attached hereto as Annex A, that negotiations should be opened for that purpose.

It is also recalled that, as there was no positive reaction on the part of the United States Government on the said matter, the Korean Government again renewed its proposal to the United States through the Foreign

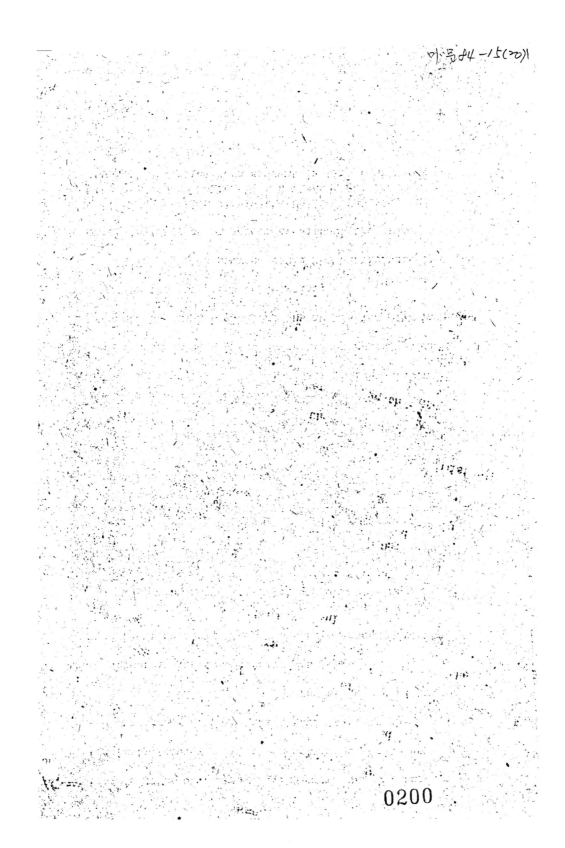

Minister's notes of January 5, 1957 and June 29, 1957 respectively, copies of which are attached hereto as Annex B and Annex C. No definite reply stating the position of the United States Government in regard to these proposals has been received as yet.

Attention is invited to the note (Annex D hereto) of General Lemnitzer of July 26, 1955 addressed to the Foreign Minister, in which the former, in expressing his views on the possibility of negotiations on the said Agreement, stated that the United States Government envisages difficulties in commencing negotiations immediately for two reasons:

1) It would be preferred by the United States Government that the negotiations for the proposed treaty of Friendship, Commerce and Navigation between the two countries as well as an agreement guaranteeing investments be completed before the initiation of negotiations for the agreement in question;

2) The Unified Command could not participate in negotiations of such an agreement without the prior consent of the allies within the Unified Command, and the task of obtaining such consent is time consuming.

0201

미문84-15
0202

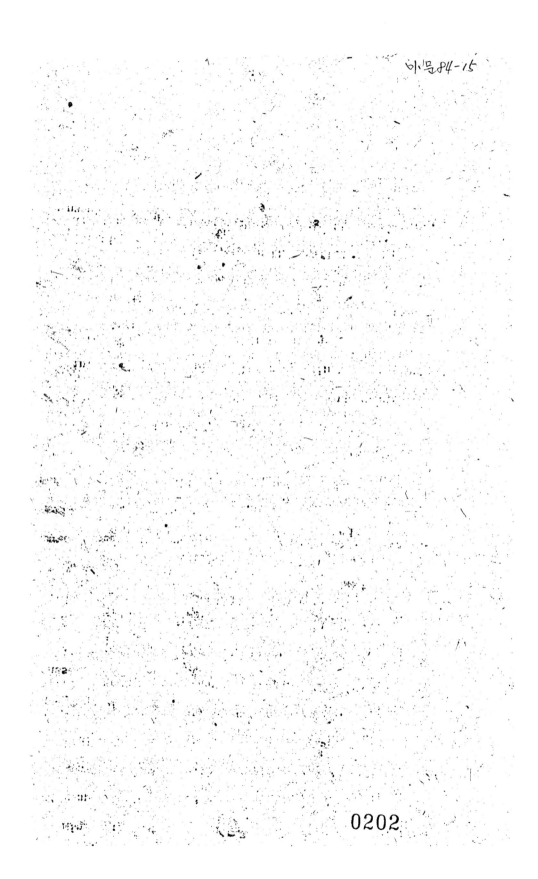

As for the first reason mentioned above, the Korea-United States Treaty of Friendship, Commerce and Navigation has been already signed and is now only awaiting exchange of the instruments of ratification. As for the agreement guaranteeing investment, i.e. the so-called MSA Guarantee Agreement proposed by the United States Government, the Korean Government is preparing the final draft, and a definite agreement should be reached in the immediate future.

As for the second reason, the Government of the Republic of Korea is of the opinion that, as the United States forces in Korea actually constitute the preponderant components of the United Nations Forces under the Unified Command, the negotiations could be commenced first between the Korean Government and the United States Government regarding the status of the United States forces in Korea.

Apart from the above-mentioned two reasons, it is presumed that the reluctance on the part of the United States Government to commence negotiations on this subject is based on the fact that Korea is technically still in a state of war. Needless to say, however, active

0203

미·무84-15
0204

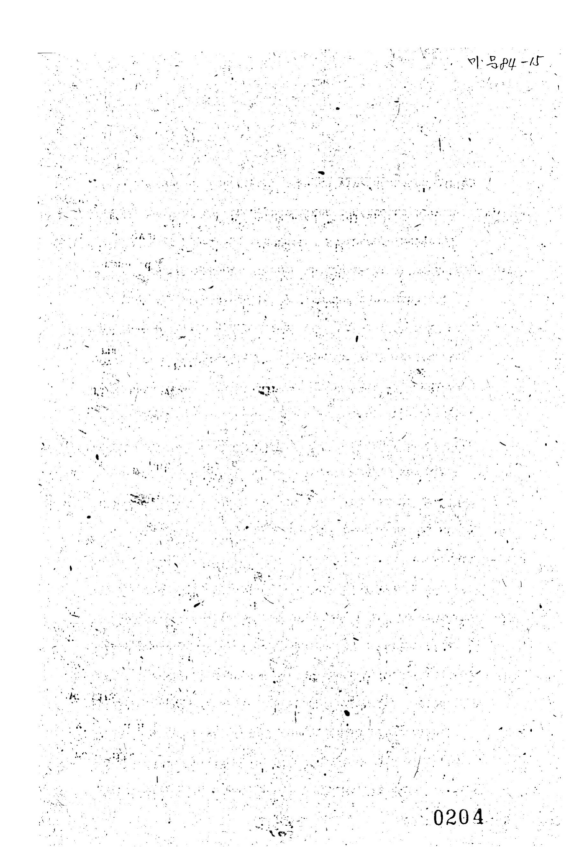

hostilities is not considered imminent. It cannot be predicted how long the current situation will last.

Under these circumstances, it is not realistic to consider the current situation, which has lasted so long, a state of war in a virtual sense. Therefore, the Korean Government does not consider that anything in the current situation in Korea prevents the Government of the Republic of Korea and the United States of America from entering into the relations which would be established if the Agreement under reference be concluded. As for the anxiety concerning the possible recurrence of hostilities in Korea, there would be no reason why the parties to the proposed Agreement should not review the applicability of the provisions concerned in such case.

What the Korean Government desires to conclude with the United States is nothing but such agreements similar to those concluded by the latter with NATO powers in 1951 and with Japan in 1952 on the same subject.

In the absence of such an agreement between the Republic of Korea and the United States of America, and in view of the then-prevailing conditions of warfare and urgent necessity, a *modus vivendi*, which partly

0205

0206

defined the status of the United States forces in Korea, came into being between the two governments through the exchange of notes at Taejon on July 12, 1950 concerning the exclusive jurisdiction by court-martial of the United States over its military personnel in Korea. In view of the changed conditions after the summer of 1953, the aofresaid provisional arrangement of 1950 is no longer appropriate in its nature nor sufficient to meet and solve adequately, under the circumstances, all of the complicated problems and matters arising daily because of the stationing and dispostion of United States forces in Korea.

In this connection, it is with regret that numerous incidents must be mentioned which occurred between the United States army personnel and local civilians; in most cases, incidents caused by delinquency on the part of members of the United States forces in Korea, involving many casualties and much damage to valuable property. All of such incidents, according to the provisional arrangement of 1950, are exclusively within the jurisdiction of the United States. The Korean Government especially fears that such incidents, and the

0207

마문84-15

0208

present way of application of justice, may injure the friendly relationship existing between the peoples of the two countries.

The Government of the Republic of Korea again requests the Government of the United States of America to give favorable consideration to the proposal of the Korean Government so that negotiations between the two governments may be commenced as early as possible. A prompt conclusion of the Agreement in question would undoubtedly serve to promote increased friendship between the peoples of the two countries.

0209

미·문84-15

0210

ANNEX A.

April 28, 1955

Dear Mr. Charge d'Affaires:

I have the honour to initiate a proposal to conclude an Administrative Agteement between the Government of the Republic of Korea and the Government of the United States of America, and enclose herewith a draft of the Agreement. With regard to this proposal, I would like first to refer to my note dated December 2, 1954, concerning a conclusion of provisional Agreement regarding the functions of Korean customs authorities with respect to the United Nations forces in Korea. Particular reference was made in the note to the effect that such customs agreement will remain in force pending conclusion of a General Administrative Agreement which shall cover other subjects also.

Having in mind that the United Nations forces under the Unified Command are and will be disposed in and about the territory of the Republic of Korea until the objective of the United Nations in Korea will have been achieved prusuant to the resolutions of the United

0211

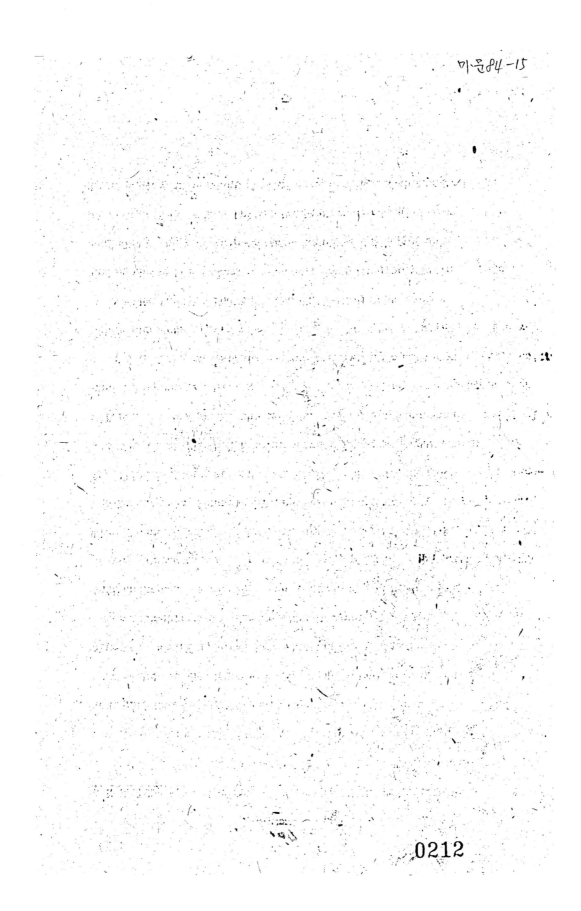

미문84-15
0212

Nations Security Council of June 25, 1950, June 27, 1950 and July 7, 1950, it is the belief of the Korean Government that terms shall be provided, for the interests of both parties, to govern the dispositon of and render convenience to the said forces in and about Korea, and that they shall be determined through mutual agreement between the Republic of Korea and the United States of America acting as the Unified Command in accordance with "The Resolution on the Settlement of the Unified Command" of the Security Council of the United Nations of July 7, 1950. A practical and effective Administrative Agreement to be concluded between the said two parties will help minimize misunderstanding and maximize cooperativeness between the Korean people and United Nations forces personnel in Korea.

In the belief that a conclusion of the Agreement is in the mutual interests, I wish to propose formally, on behalf of the Government of the Republic of Korea, that negotiation will be commenced between the representatives of Korean Government and the United States Government. Upon the receipt of your consent, we will proceed to decide the date and place of the conference,

0213

마음84-15
0214

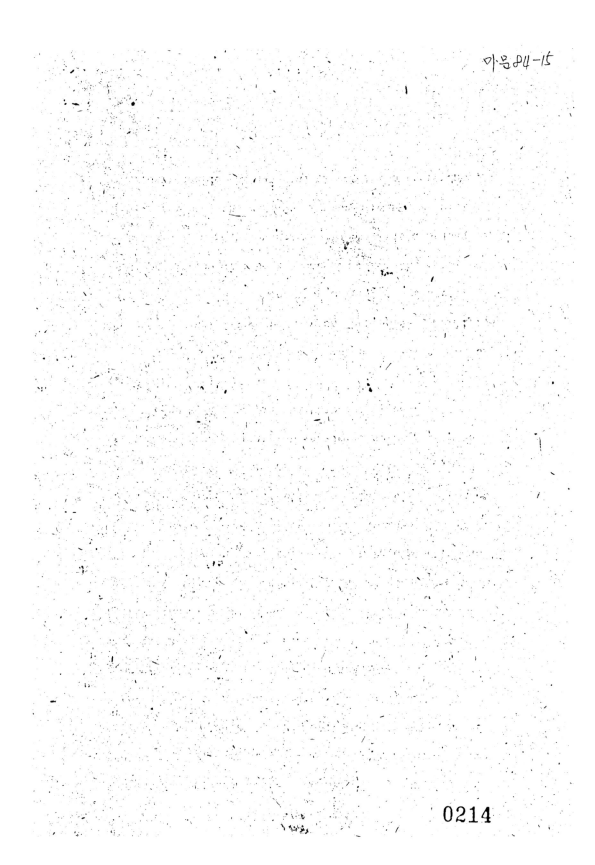

which will be mutually agreeable.

Accept, dear Mr. Charge d'Affaires, the assurnaces of my highest consideration.

Enclosure: Draft of Administrative
Ageement

/s/

Y. T. Pyun
Minister of
Foreign Affairs

The Honourable Carl W. Strom,
Charge d'Affaires,
Embassy of the United States of America
Seoul, Korea

0215

미·문84-15
0216

ANNEX B.

January 5, 1957

Excellency:

I have the honour to refer to the Foreign Minister's note addressed to Mr. Carl W. Strom, Charge d'Affairs ad interim of the Embassy of the United States of America in Korea dated April 28, 1955 enclosing a draft of an Administrative Agreement between the Republic of Korea and the Unified Command for establishment of the Status of the United Nations Forces in Korea.

In the afore-said note, the Minister informed the Government of the United States of America of the desire of the Korean Government to commence negotiations with the United States Government for the said Status of Forces Agreement which will also define the former's customs functions as referred to in my letter of December 2, 1954.

To this proposal, however, no acceptance

0217

미문84-15

0218

has been given as yet, although the American Charge d'Affairs notified in his replying note of May 9, 1955, that upon obtaining his Government's view on the said request, he would communicate with the Minister.

I hereby wish again to propose, on behalf of my Government, that negotiation be commenced at an earliest possible date between the representatives of the Korean Government and the United States Government. In connection with this re-proposal, I would like further to refer to the note of July 26, 1955 addressed to the Foreign Minister by General Lemnitzer advising on this matter.

General Lemnitzer expressed his views on the possibility of negotiating the said agreement in the above note to the effect that the United States Government envisages difficulties in commencing immediately negotiations for a proposed agreement for the following two reasons:

The one reason was that it would be

0219

미·문84-15

0220

preferable to the American Government that negotiations for a proposed treaty of Friendship, Commerce and Navigation between the two countries as well as an agreement guaranteeing investments be completed before the initiation of negotiation for an agreement in question. The other was that the Unified Command cannot participate in negotiation of such agreement without the prior consent of allies within the Unified Command and it is anticipated that the task of obtaining such consent will be difficult.

Attention, however, is paid to the fact that the points indicated above constitute no longer difficulties about negotiating the said agreement under the present circumstances.

The Treaty of Friendship, Commerce and Navigation has been already signed and is now waiting to be formally ratified. As regards the agreement guaranteeing investments, discussions have been completed on provisions of its draft and now the work of finalising it remains

0221

미동84-75

0222

only. On the other hand, since allies within the Unified Command have been decreased in number into twelve nations and since the American forces form the predominant components of the United Nations forces, there exist no difficulties, it is believed, in securing consent of other allies as to the matter.

And thus, even in case the consent of the other allies has not been obtained as yet, it is, therefore, proposed that negotiations be started first between both represnetatives of the Korean Government and the United States Government and that negotiations with other allies shall be carried on separately in accordance with terms to be agreed upon between Korea and the United States of America. It is sincerely requested that the concurrence of the United States Government be given to the wish of the Korean Government to commence negotiations for the agreement proposed.

Please accept, Excellency, the renewed assurances of my highest consideration.

0223

미문84-15

0224

/s/

Chung W. Cho
Minister of
Foreign Affairs

His Excellency
The right honourable
Walter C. Dowling
Ambassador of the United States
of America to the Republic of Korea
Seoul, Korea

0225

미문84-15
0226

ANNEX C.

June 29, 1957

My dear Mr. Ambassador:

I have the honor to remind your Government, as I have orally mentioned to you on several occasions, that the conclusion of an Administrative Agreement defining and setting forth in detail the status of United States troops stationed in Korea is still pending.

On April 28, 1955, our draft proposal of an Administrative Agreement between this Government and the Unified Command, to establish the status of United Nations forces in Korea, was addressed to your Embassy. On November 1, 1956, it was proposed that a separate agreement be negotiated between representatives of this Government and the United States Government, in case of difficulty in obtaining early consent of the other Allied Govern-

미일84-15
0228

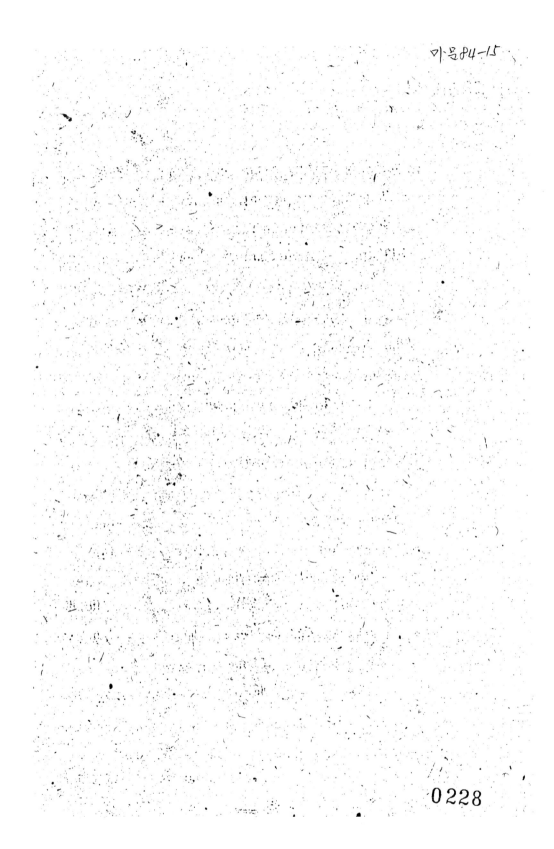

ments.

In the absence of such an administrative agreement, a temporary agreement was made through the exchange of Notes at Taejon, on July 12, 1950, concerning the exclusive jurisdiction by court-martial of the United States over members of the United States Military Establishment in Korea. This agreement, which is still in force, was improvised to meet an emergency situation and is not considered sufficient to meet effectively all the complex and complicated problems arising from the presence of United States troops in Korea.

This Government is strongly convinced that the early conclusion of a formal and detailed agreement on the status of United States troops in Korea would serve to strengthen cordial relations between our people and American military personnel, and would provide great satisfaction to the mutual cause and interest of both countries.

0229

미문84-15

0230

I wish to state again that this Government is most desirous of receiving the concurrence of the United States Government in order to commence negotiations for an administrative agreement along the lines of the proposal of April, 1955. Your Government's earliest favorable consideration of this matter is most sincerely desired.

Accept, Excellency, renewed assurances of my highest consideration.

/s/

Chung W. Cho
Minister

His Excellency
Ambassador Walter C. Dowling
American Embassy,
Seoul.

0231

미올84-15

0232

ANNEX D.

26 July 1955

Dear Minister Pyun:

Thank you very much for your letter of 13 June 1955, in which you acknowledge receipt of General Taylor's letter of 14 May 1955, with the inclosures pertaining to customs functions of the Republic of Korea.

I have noted the desire of the Korean Government to commence negotiations with the Government of the United States for a Status of Forces Agreement between the Korean Government and the Unified Command. This matter is presently under study by the Departments of my government in Washington.

Current thinking on this matter is that it would be preferable that negotiations now in progress or pending be completed before the initiation of negotiations

미무84-15

0234

for an agreement of the type in question. Ambassador Lacy advises me that a proposed treaty of friendship, commerce and navigation between our respective governments is under consideration, as well as an agreement guaranteeing investments, and that he is anxious to complete these matters before taking up any other major negotiations.

I am sure you are also aware that the Unified Command cannot participate in a negotiation of any Status of Forces Agreement without the prior consent of our allies within the United Nations Command. It is anticipated that the task of obtaining this consent will be difficult and time consuming.

Sincerely,

/s/

L.L. LEMNITZER
General, United
States Army,
Commander-in-Chief

0235

미명84-15

0236

His Excellency Pyun Yung-Tai

Minister of Foreign Affairs of

The Republic of Korea

0237

미문84-15(20)

0238

16. Foreign Minister's letter of November 13, 1957 to the United States Ambassador.

November 13, 1957

Dear Mr. Ambassador:

I wish to bring to your attention the question of an Agreement on the status of the United States Forces in Korea and to recent developments in our efforts to solve problems arising between members of the United States Forces and Korean nationals.

Since the cessation of active hostilities in 1953, it has become increasingly clear that a modus vivendi reached between our two Governments through an exchange of notes at Taejon on July 12, 1950 allowing the United States exclusive

His Excellency
Walter C. Dowling,
Ambassador,
American Embassy,
Seoul.

0239

0240

jurisdiction by court-martial of members of the United States Forces in Korea is not sufficient to cope with various complicated problems involving members of the United States Forces and our people.

This Government, keenly desiring to conclude an agreement on the status of United States Forces in our Country, initially proposed to your Government through the Foreign Minister's note of April 28, 1955, that negotiations be commenced for that purpose, and later, having failed to receive any positive reaction to this proposal, brought up the matter again on several occasions. When the Under Secretary of State visited Korea, a note on this question dated September 10, 1957, was presented to Mr. Herter in the hope that the matter would receive his favorable attention. A copy of this note is enclosed.

In this connection, I am deeply

0241

미문84-16
0242

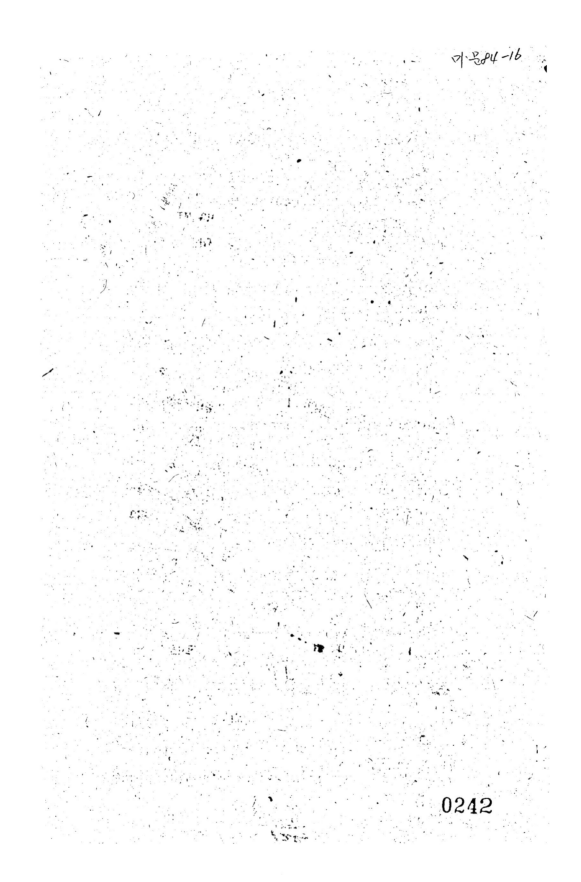

interested in a suggestion made by you at a meeting held in my office on October 10, 1957 that "there might be room for reaching a separate agreement on particular items as was done in the unitities problems." I deeply appreciate your friendly and co-operative interest in these problems and will be very happy to proceed with negotiations for separate agreements with your Government on particular items; for instance, taxation, customs duty, and criminal jurisdiction. I am confident such negotiations will lead to an acceptable solution to our common problems.

With warmest personal regards, I remain

sincerely yours,

/s/

Chung W. Cho
Minister

Enclosure: as stated.

0243

미·무84-16(3)

0244

17. Foreign Minister's letter of November 26, 1957 to the United States Charge d'Affaires, and the enclosed memorandum concerning the ROK Government's position on the negotiation of separate agreements on various subjects pertaining to the status of United States forces in Korea.

November 26, 1957

Dear Mr. Charge d'Affaires:

I refer to my letter of November 13, 1957, addressed to Ambassador Dowling, regarding the agreement on the status of United States forces in Korea. In this letter I suggested we commence negotiations to conclude separate agreements on particular items such as taxation, customs duties, etc., instead of concluding a full-scale agreement.

In this connection, I have pleasure in forwarding a memorandum on the position of my Government on the separate agreements to be concluded between our two Governments.

It would be greatly appreciated if

0245

미.모84-17(8)
0246

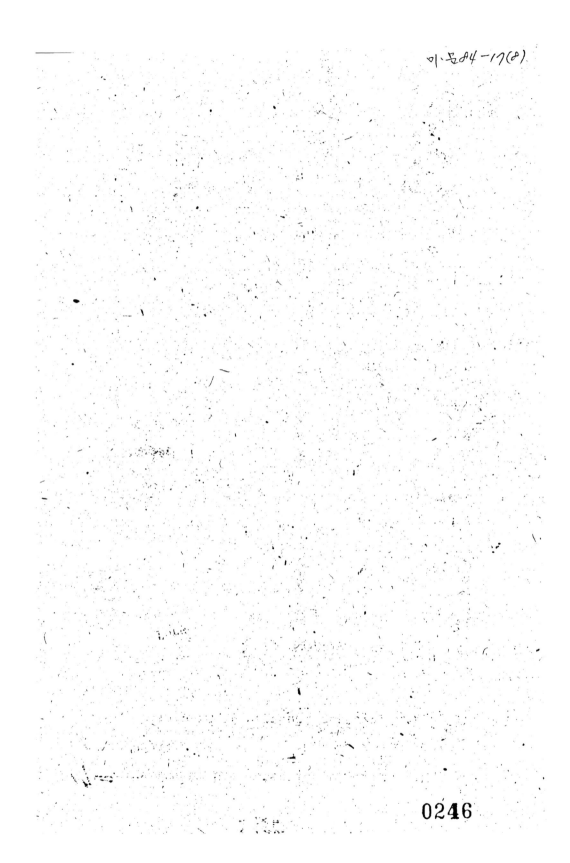

you give favourable attention to this memorandum.

With warmest personal regards, I remain

Sincerely yours,

/s/

Chung W. Cho
Minister

Mr. T. Eliot Weil,
Charge d'Affaires, a.i.,
American Embassy,
Seoul.

0247

0248

MEMORANDUM

Considering the present stalemate which exists between Korea and the United States regarding the commencement of negotiations for the conclusion of a full-scale administrative agreement to govern the entire status of United States forces in Korea, it is recommended that several agreements between the two Governments be separately concluded so that the status of United States forces in Korea can be regulated as far as possible upon a mutually acceptable basis:

1) Agreement concerning Procurement, Taxation and Customs Duties of United States forces in Korea. (Ref. Art. 6, 7, 8 of Draft Administrative Agreement proposed by the Korean Government.)

2) Agreement concerning Settlement of Claims relative to the stationing of United States forces in Korea. (Ref. Art. 5)

0249

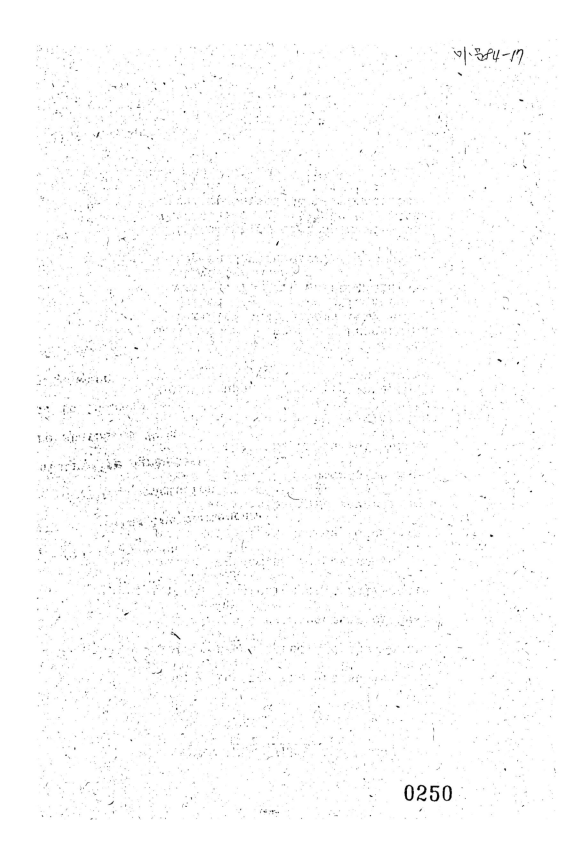

3) Agreement concerning Facilities and Areas to be used by United States forces in Korea. (Ref. Art. 3, para. 10 of Art. 4, Art. 9, 10)

4) Agreement concerning Entry and Exit of United States forces in Korea. (Ref. Art. 2)

5) Agreement concerning Criminal Jurisdiction over Offences by United States forces in Korea. (Ref. Art. 4, 13, 14)

1. Agreement concerning Procurement, Taxation and Customs Duties of United States forces in Korea.

It is vital for the Republic of Korea Government to check the smuggling conducted through the supply routes of United States forces in Korea. This agreement is one of the most urgent to be concluded between the two countries. For the purpose of preventing and checking the aforesaid smuggling, the Korean Customs Officials wish to have access, for inspection purposes, to the wharves and military airports, which

0251

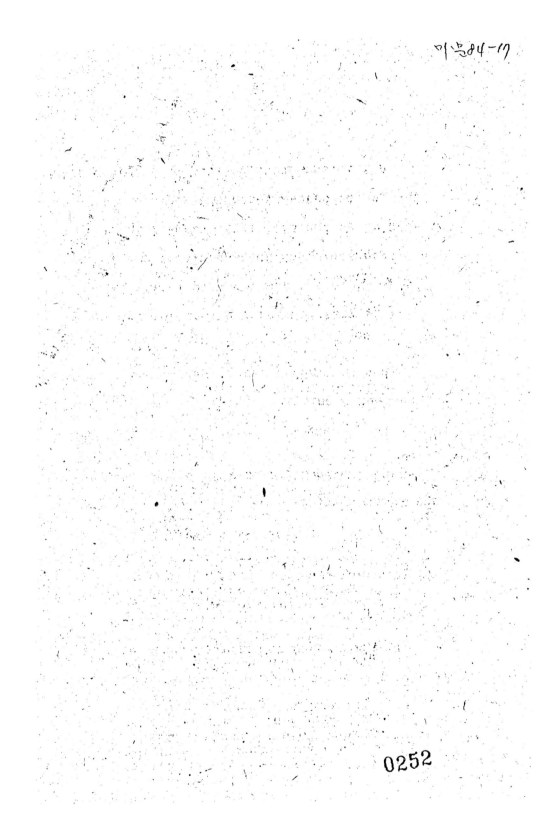

are now exclusively held and controlled by the United States military authorities.

As for procurements, goods and services which are required and can be obtained from local sources for the subsistance of United States forces should be procured in a manner most likely to help maintain Korean economic stability, and least probable of adversely affecting it, also in coordination with and, when desirable, through or with the assistance of competent authorities of Korea.

2. Agreement concerning Settlement of Claims relative to United States forces in Korea.

This agreement is to govern civil jurisdiction, particularly the settlement of claims arising out of injuries and damages to Korean nationals and their properties caused by United States forces, and to facilitate settlement of the claims

0253

0254

arising out of such injuries and damages. On the other hand, the Korean Government will undertake to make every effort to protect United States forces and their members from injuries to them and damage to their properties.

3. Agreement concerning Facilities and Areas to be used by United States forces in Korea.

While the Korean Government is willing to grant to United States forces the use of certain facilities and areas and certain rights, powers and authority necessary for carrying out their mission, this agreement is aimed to clarify the scope of exemption from the liabilities of compensation or restoration accruing from the use of such facilities and areas.

This agreement will also contain provisions in regard to military post office

0255

미북84-17

0256

and non-appropriated fund organizations, and further, such provisions as will enable the Korean Government to make interim use of any of such facilities or areas of target ranges and maneuver grounds, which are temporarily not used by United States forces.

4. Agreement concerning Entry and Exit of United States forces in Korea.

This agreement will clarify the scope of exemption from Korean immigration laws and regulations for the members of United States forces, including civilian components and their dependents.

5. Agreement concerning Criminal Jurisdiction over Offences by United States forces in Korea.

It is to propose to the United States Government to amend the existing Taejon/

0257

agreement of 1950 to suit the changed conditojs caused by the cessation of actual hostilities. As for the amendment, efforts should be made to limit the jurisdiction of the United States court-martial over members of United States forces to such cases as have occurred in the course of execution of official duties, and further to make additional provisions for judicial cooperation, including joint search and investigation.

Ministry of Foreign Affairs
Seoul, Korea

November 26, 1957

0259

미문84-17(8)
0260

18. United States Charge d'Affaires' reply of December 3, 1957 to the Foreign Minister's letter of November 26, 1957.

American Embassy,
Seoul, Korea,
December 3, 1957.

My dear Mr. Minister:

I have the honor to acknowledge receipt of your letter of November 26, 1957 with which was enclosed a memorandum concerning the position of your Government on the question of negotiating separate agreements on various subjects pertaining to the status of United States forces in Korea.

I have forwarded copies of your letter and enclosure to Washington for consideration by my Government.

I shall hope, in due course, to send you a further communication on the subject

0261

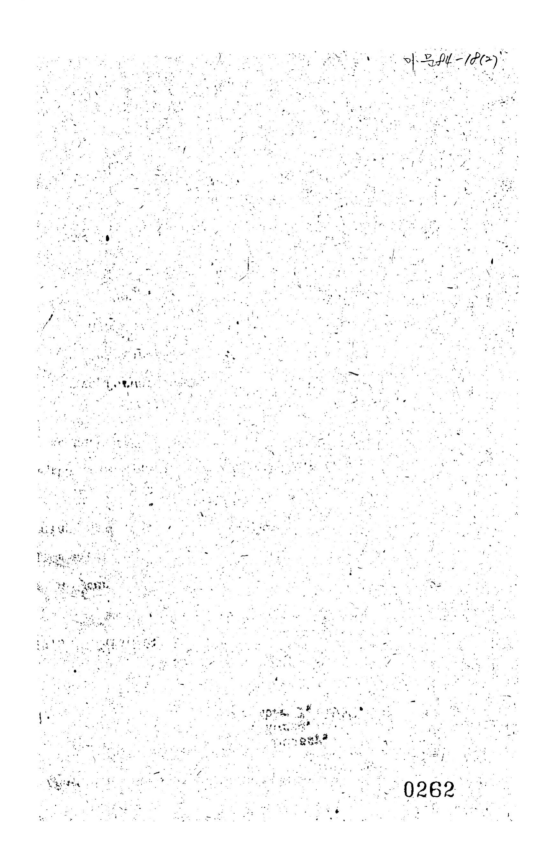

of your Government's memorandum.

With warmest personal regards, I am

Sincerely yours,

/s/

T. Eliot Weil
Charge d'Affaires ad interim

His Excellency
Chung W. Cho
Minister of Foreign Affairs,
Republic of Korea.

0263

미·문84-18121

0264

19. Memorandum for the Office of the President 0380

MEMORANDUM KPO/101

September 18, 1958

MEMORANDUM FOR THE OFFICE OF THE PRESIDENT[1]

1. U.S. Ambassador Walter C. Dowling called on Vice-Foreign Minister Dong Jo Kim at the latter's office at 5:00 p.m., September 18, 1958 to convey the view of the Department of State on the issue of the proposed Agreement on Status of U.S. Forces in Korea, which has been pending since these four years between the two Governments.

2. Before entering discussion on the main subject, Mr. Dowling wanted to exchange views on prospect of the Korea-Japan talks though he expressed nothing new. Then, he stated that U.S. Secretary of State Dulles, in his speech made at the U.N. forum today, delivered U.S. viewpoints straight out particularly on

---

1. This Memorandum was orally presented by Vice-Foreign Minister Dong Jo Kim to His Excellency the President on September 19, 1958 at Kyung Mu Dai. His Excellency disapproved the "Points of View" contained in the said Memorandum. His Excellency stated that we should request an agreement on 'jurisdiction'.

0265 78-21-3

58-21-3 (5)

0266

0308

the problems of admission of the Republic of Korea into the United Nations, Formosa straits situation, etc.

3. Turning to the main subject, Ambassador Dowling delivered the following points of view from Washington:

A) Though there is no actual shooting now in Korea, the current situation is rather deemed as a state of cessation of hostilities, complete state of peace being yet to be resumed. Under this situation, time has not yet come when the two Governments have talks to define status of forces under the United Nations Command, accordingly, what is related to jurisdiction of the said Command.

B) However, this is not to prevent the two Governments from exploring the possibility of reaching agreements on such problems as of purely administrative nature, unless it touches upon the problem of the 'jurisdiction of the Command' [by the term, 'jurisdiction' he had in mind 'criminal jurisdiction']; such problems may include enforcement of customs regulations, taxation, entry and exit of personnel, etc.

0267

58-21-4

58-21-3

미.문84-1

0268

C) After an exploratory talks for defining the scope of terms, agreements may be reached in the form of Memorandum of Understanding, Exchange of Notes and so on, and such agreements would surely serve further promotion of friendly relations existing between the two nations.

D) But, the U.S. side is suggesting the above on condition that the Korean side will not further propose negotiation for an agreement on jurisdiction of the Command, as next step. so long as the present circumstances in Korea continue to prevail; therefore, if the negotiation is to be commenced, the U.S. desires that the two Governments issue a Joint Statement to put in record a clear-cut understanding to that effect.

E) He (Ambassador Dowling) is now authorized to start talks with the Korean side for this purpose; if the Korean side concurs with U.S., negotiation can be commenced after his return from trip to Japan which will be made from 21 to 25 September 1958.

4. Vice-Minister Kim told Mr. Dowling that he would study the U.S. suggestion.

58 — 의 — 3

0270

0346

POINTS OF VIEW

1. It has been our anxious desire to expedite the conclusion of Agreement on Status of U.S. Forces in Korea since we first proposed it to the United States in 1954. From the beginning, the proposal was not favorably reacted. But it has been also our policy to settle even partially the problems which arise from the stationing of foreign armed forces in Korea.

2. Therefore, the U.S. suggestion conveyed by Ambassador Dowling on September 18, 1958 marked a step forward in the direction of the settlement of the problem long-pending between the two Governments. There is no reason why we should not respond to the U.S. suggestion.

3. However, it is not advisable for our Government to join the U.S. in issuing a statement to the effect that we will never enter talks for conclusion of agreement on criminal jurisdiction of U.S. military personnel, because it may bring a great disappointment to our people while such statement is tantamount to perpetuating legally the validity of Korea-U.S. Agreement on Criminal

0271

18-21-6

0272

0340

Jurisdiction of U.S. Military Personnel which was signed at Taejon in July, 1950.

4. In view of the above, it would be advisable for us to commence talks by assuring orally what the U.S. wishes to be assured instead of issuing a Joint Statement.

0273

58-21-7

58 - 21 - 3 (5)

미·무84-1P(15)

0274

0550

20. Memorandum for the Office of the President on negotiation for an agreement on the facilities and areas in use by U.S. forces in Korea

RECOMMENDATION KPO/186

May 12, 1959

TO : His Excellency the President

FROM : Foreign Minister

SUBJECT : Proposal to Start Negotiations for the Conclusion of Agreement concerning the Facilities and Areas to be Used by the U.S. Forces in Korea

In view of the fact that the absence of an equitable agreement on the status of U.S. forces in Korea has caused various difficulties in the relations of U.S. forces and local Korean populace, the Government has repeatedly requested the U.S. Government to conclude an Agreement which will regulate the status of U.S. forces in Korea.

The reaction of the U.S. Government, however, has been dilatory toward our repeated requests and no negotiation for conclusion of the above-mentioned agreement has been undertaken despite of our earnest efforts on the question. The main reason for the U.S. reluctancy to conclude a comprehensive Status of Forces

0275 5P-19-2

59-18-2(6)

미문 pll-20(6)

0276

0538

Agreement with the Republic of Korea seems to be stemming from the U.S. hesitancy to turn over to the Korean authorities a part of its jurisdictional rights over U.S. military personnel stationed in Korea, which it enjoys now by virtue of existing agreement between the two Governments.

Although the best policy of our Government is to conclude a comprehensive Status of Forces Agreement with the U.S. side to regulate all problems arising from the stationing in Korea of U.S. forces, and early settlement of this question at the present time is not likely due to the above-mentioned attitude of the U.S. side. Under the circumstances, the Ministry finds it advisable to settle problems first on item-by-item basis for it would better the interests of our Government. As a matter of fact, such item-by-item approach has already been employed by the Ministry when it concluded, for instance, agreements on the problems of U.S. surplus property and on the public utilities for the U.S. forces in Korea.

The first item that should be dealt with is an agreement on the facilities and lands that are used by the U.S. forces in Korea.

58-18-4

0277

59-18-2

0278

0380

If the recommendation meets with Your Excellency's approval, the Ministry will send a note, the draft of which is attached herewith, to Ambassador Dowling and its copy to General Decker, proposing to commence negociations for conclusion of an agreement on the said subject.

Most respectfully,

0279

58-10-5

59-18-2

미·동24-20

0280

 0388

/D R A F T/

Excellency,

I have the honor to draw your attention to the subject of usage of the facilities and areas now in use by the U.S. forces in Korea.

As you may recall, most of the facilities and areas presently in use by the U.S. forces in Korea were furnished by the Korean authorities under the emergency state during and immediately after the outbreak of the Korean War. Under the then prevailing situation, no adequate agreement was concluded between the Government of the Republic of Korea and the Government of the United States of America to regulate various problems in relation to the use of facilities and areas by the U.S. forces in Korea.

Under the present circumstances, my Government feels that it would best serve the interests of both countries that are wholeheartedly engaged in their joint efforts against the common enemy if the two Governments conclude an equitable agreement concerning the facilities and areas that are used by the U.S. forces in Korea. In view of the fact that the absence

0281 5P-18-6

59-18-2

미·드84-20

0282

of such an agreement in the past made it impossible to settle problems related to the use of facilities and areas by the U.S. forces stationed in Korea, an agreement of this nature would ensure the joint defense efforts of the two Governments to be very fruitful and most satisfactory.

I wish to propose, therefore, that the representatives of both the Korean and U.S. Governments meet and discuss for conclusion of an agreement which would cover at least the following points:

(1) The Korean Government will endeavor to materialize in the proposed agreement regulations to enable the United States forces in Korea to carry out their operation in most effective way;

(2) Both Governments will review the conditions by which the U.S. forces are using the facilities and areas in Korea; but the Korean Government will grant, in accordance with international precedents, the continued use by the United States forces of the facilities and areas presently in use; and

(3) The United States Government will give due consideration to owners of the properties offered to them.

0283 58-10-17

59-18-2

0588

미공84-20

0284

I sincerely hope that the above proposal of my Government will receive favorable consideration by your Government and that on that basis the negotiations be commenced for conclusion of an agreement on the subject matter at an earliest date.

Accept, Excellency, the renewed assurances of my highest consideration.

/s/
Chung W. Cho
Minister

His Excellency
Walter C. Dowling
Ambassador of the United States
of America

58-10-8

59-18-2 (6)

미. 동811-70 (6)

0392

0286

21. Foreign Minister's note of June 10, 1959 to the United States Ambassador, proposing an agreement on the facilities and areas in use by U.S. forces

June 10, 1959

Excellency,

I have the honor to draw your attention to the subject of usage of the facilities and areas now in use by the U.S. forces in Korea.

As you may recall, most of the facilities and areas presently in use by the U.S. forces in Korea were furnished by the Korean authorities under the emergency state during and immediately after the outbreak of the Korean War. Under the then prevailing situation, no adequate agreement was concluded between the Government of the Republic of Korea and the Government of the United States of America to regulate various problems in relation to these facilities.

My Government feels that it would best serve the interests of both countries that are wholeheartedly engaged in their joint efforts against the common enemy if the two Governments conclude an equitable agreement regarding the same. In view of the fact

59-18-3

미음84-21(3)

0288

that the absence of such an agreement in the past made it impossible to resolve problems related to the use of such facilities and areas, an agreement of this nature would improve the defense efforts of the two Governments.

I wish to propose, therefore, that the representatives of both the Korean and U.S. Government meet and discuss and later conclude such an agreement which could cover (1) regulations to enable the United States forces in Korea to carry out their operation in a most effective way; (2) set out the conditions under which the U.S. forces will be using the facilities and areas involved; (3) with the Korean Government granting, in accordance with international precedents, the continued use by the United States forces of such facilities and areas and (4) with the United States Government giving full consideration to owners of the properties.

I sincerely hope that the above will receive favorable consideration by your Government and that discussions could be commenced at the earliest date possible with end in view of concluding an agreement along the lines indicated above, without delay.

58-18-17

59-18-3

마-문84-21

0290

0585

Accept, Excellency, the renewed assurances of my highest consideration.

Chung W. Cho
Minister

His Excellency
Walter C. Dowling
Ambassador of the United States of America

0291

59-18-3 (5)

미문84-21(3)

0292

22\. The United States Ambassador's reply of June 15, 1959 to the Foreign Minister's note of June 10, 1959

Seoul, June 15, 1959.

No. 983

Excellency:

I have the honor to refer to Your Excellency's note of June 10, 1959, proposing negotiation and conclusion of an agreement on the usage of facilities and areas now in use by United States Forces in Korea.

I also have the honor to inform Your Excellency that I have forwarded your proposal to the Department of State for its consideration.

Accept, Excellency, the renewed assurances of my highest consideration.

/s/
Walter Dowling

His Excellency
Cho Chong-hwan,
Minister of Foreign Affairs,
Seoul.

59-18-20

59-18-4 (3)

0303

미유 84-22

0294

23. The Acting Foreign Minister's note of October 15, 1959 to the United States Chargé d'Affaires ad interim

PT-21

The Acting Minister of Foreign Affairs presents his compliments to the Chargé d'Affaires ad interim of the United States of America and has the honor to refer to the Foreign Minister's note of June 10, 1959, proposing negotiation for conclusion of an agreement on the usage of facilities and areas now in use by United States forces in Korea.

The Acting Minister would be grateful if the Chargé d'Affaires ad interim would meet promptly the desire of the Government of the Republic of Korea to commence the proposed negotiation.

The Acting Minister avails himself of this opportunity to renew to the Chargé d'Affaires ad interim of the United States of America the assurances of his high consideration.

October 15, 1959
Seoul

59-18-21

0295

59-18-5(1)

0296

0298

24. A letter of October 29, 1959 from Minister Pyo Wook Han, Korean Embassy in Washington D. C., to the Vice Minister of Foreign Affairs

KOREAN EMBASSY

Washington, D. C.

October 29, 1959

Dear Minister Choi,

Enclosed is a copy of a memorandum prepared by Mr. Chyun, our First Secretary, with reference to the agreement on the usage of facilities and areas now in use by U.S. forces in Korea.

Sincerely yours,

/s/
Pyo Wook Han
Minister

The Honorable
Kyu Ha Choi
Vice Minister
Seoul, Republic of Korea

Enclosure - 1

5P-18-24

0297 —→

59-18-6(4)

미문84-24(4)

0298

MEMORANDUM

TO : Minister Han

FROM : First Secretary Sang jin Chyun

SUBJECT : Proposed conclusion of an agreement on the usage of facilities and areas now in use by U.S. forces in Korea.

In accordance with your instructions, I called on Mr. Samuel O. Lane, Chief of the Korean Desk, State Department, on Wednesday October 21, to convey our Government's desire to commence promptly the proposed negotiation for the subject agreement pursuant to the Foreign Ministry instructions dated October 15.

I reminded Mr. Lane of the fact that more than three months time had elapsed since the Korean Government formally proposed the conclusion to the American Embassy in Korea, of an "agreement on the usage of facilities and areas now in use by the U.S. forces in Korea", and urged the prompt acceptance by the U.S. Government of our long pending proposal.

In this regard, the Minister of Foreign Affairs sent a note proposing negotiations for conclusion of an agreement on the above subject to the American Ambassador

59-10-25

59-18-6

0300

in Korea on June 10, 1959 and on October 15 the Acting Foreign Minister sent another note to the American Charge d'Affaires urging the U.S. acceptance of our proposal.

Mr. Lane told me that at present the Korean proposal is under active consideration by the authorities of the State and Defense Departments. However, he was not in a position to predict a definite date for reply by the United States Government since the United States decision on the proposed agreement would depend upon its general policy with regard to the conclusion of an over all status forces agreement with Korea. The U.S. Government is of the opinion that it would be inevitable to discuss other agreements concerning several subjects on the status of U.S. forces in Korea after the conclusion of the particular agreement now in question. And to the general policy of the U.S. Government on the conclusion of a status of forces agreement with Korea even excluding the subject of criminal jurisdiction there still exists differences of opinion among responsible officials.

5P-18 -26

0301

However, the State Department officials are generally sympathetic toward the Korean position and are trying to have a decision on the proposed agreement within a month if possible.

I have cabled to the Foreign Ministry the result of my meeting with Mr. Lane as attached.

59-18-6 (4)

0305 미문84-24(4)

0304

정/리/보/존/문/서/목/록					
기록물종류	문서-일반공문서철	등록번호	942 9615	등록일자	2006-07-27
분류번호	741.12	국가코드	US	주제	
문서철명	한.미국 간의 상호방위조약 제4조에 의한 시설과 구역 및 한국에서의 미국군대의 지위에 관한 협정 (SOFA) 전59권. 1966.7.9 서울에서 서명 : 1967.2.9 발효 (조약 232호) *원본				
생산과	미주과/조약과	생산년도	1952 - 1967	보존기간	영구
담당과(그룹)	조약	조약	서가번호	--	
참조분류					
권차명	V.44 SOFA 협정 체결교섭 관련 한.미국간 수교 공한, 1952-60				
내용목차	* 일지 : 1953.8.7 이승만 대통령-Dulles 미국 국무장관 공동성명 - 상호방위조약 발효 후 군대지위협정 교섭 약속 1954.12.2 정부, 주한 UN군의 관세업무협정 체결 제의 1955.1월, 5월 미국, 제의 거절 1955.4.28 정부, 군대지위협정 제의 (한국측 초안 제시) 1957.9.10 Hurter 미국 국무차관 방한 시 각서 수교 (한국측 제의 수락 요구) 1957.11.13, 26 정부, 개별 협정의 단계적 체결 제의 1958.9.18 Dawling 주한미국대사, 형사재판관할권 협정 제외 조건으로 행정협정 체결 의사 전달 1960.3.10 정부, 토지, 시설협정의 우선적 체결 강력 요구 1961.4.10 장면 국무총리-McConaughy 주한미국대사 공동성명으로 교섭 개시 합의 1961.4.15, 4.25 제1, 2차 한.미국 교섭회의 (서울) 1962.3.12 정부, 교섭 재개 촉구 공한 송부 1962.5.14 Burger 주한미국대사, 최규하 장관 면담 시 형사재판관할권 문제 제기 않는 조건으로 교섭 재개 통고 1962.9.6 한.미국 간 공동성명 발표 (9월 중 교섭 재개 합의) 1962.9.20~ 1965.6.7 제1-81차 실무 교섭회의 (서울) 1966.7.8 제82차 실무 교섭회의 (서울) 1966.7.9 서명 1967.2.9 발효 (조약 232호)					

마/이/크/로/필/름/사/항				
촬영연도	*롤 번호	화일 번호	후레임 번호	보관함 번호
2006-11-24	I-06-0071	04	1-85	

0001

Chornologically Collected Official Notes on
ADMINISTRATIVE AGREEMENT BETWEEN ROK-USA

1952.11.18 - 57.2.4

관리번호 43

검토필(1962.12.7.)

검토필(196.4.12.30.)

검토필(1965.6.30.)

일반문서로 재분류 (협정체결시)

일반문서로 재분류 협정체결시

487

17P

0002

0003

永久保存

條約

件名

(全英文名)

四二八年 月 日 署名
四二八年 月 日 批准
四二八年 月 日 發效
四二八年 月 日 公布

(條約第 號)

卷第 號
第 號

外務部

條約(件名) 第 卷第 號

政務局第二課文書
一連番號( )

HEADQUARTERS
KOREAN BASE SECTION
Office of the Commanding General
APO 59

Honorable S.K.Kim
Minister of Transportation
Republic of Korea
Pusan, Korea

새보추
1952. 2. 15

Dear Mr. Kim:

1. In an attempt to reach a mutually satisfactory solution to the problem of replacing Japanese personnel and equipment with Korean, the following program is proposed to meet the needs of the United Nations Command and the Republic of Korea.

a. Replacement of Japanese personnel employed on United States vessels and equipment afloat.

(1) The ROK Government, or an agency, thereof, will nominate to this headquarters complete crews for vessels or equipment according to unit lists to made available by this headquarters. Each vessel or piece of equipment is considered as a unit for this purpose. Each nominee must be technically qualified for the position to which he is nominated, licensed in an acceptable form and in possession of credentials and identification acceptable to this headquarters.

(2) Nominated unit personnel will be made available to representatives of this headquarters for test of equalifications or skills and may be rejected as lacking proper qualifications at the discretion of such representatives.

(3) Following acceptance of a unit crew as qualified by this headquarters the employer of the personnel concerned shall negotiate a contract with the Contracting Officer, Korean Base Section referred to herein as a unit per day. The employer must be a corporation or other legal entity acceptable to the Contracting Officer as a contracting party. Contracts will be subject to all terms and conditions requred by the Contracting Officer for service contracts, will be based upon the customary wage of maritime contract workers in Korea, will include customary allowance for welfare taxes and other overhead charges not to exceed 25%, and shall recite payments in won. Contracts shall provide that direction of the vessel shall be at the sole discretion of the Contracting Officer; that upon requestof the Contracting Officer a master of any member of the crew shall be discharged or disciplined; that hire of all employees shall be on a temporary

0004

118

of the contract shall be deemed to be an emplpyee of the United States, or any of its agencies or instrumentalities for any purpose whatsoever and that this stipulation shall be a part of the ship's articiles or the articles of employment. The execution administration and continuance of the contract will be within the complete and sole discretion of the Contracting officer.

(4) When, as and if the unit personnel are nominated, tested, accepted by this headquarters, and a contract is approved and executed, Japanese personnel of the unit concerned shall be released subject to the paramount requirements of efficient and uninterrupted operations.

b. Replacement of Japanese personnel and Japanese owned or operated vessels and equipment by Korea personnel and Korean owned or operated vessels and equipment.

(1) The provisions of subparagraph la (1) and (2) shall apply.

(2) The ROK government agrees to locate all available vessels and equipment similar in size and function to those intended to be replaced as indicated on lists to be made available by this headquarters, and will effect direct, completive negotiations with the owners to the exclution of brokers. Selected bessels will be released to this headquarters for inspection and test of suitability at the expense of the owner, the acceptability of any vessel being within the sole discretion of this headquarters.

(3) Following acceptance of a unit and crew as qualified by this headquarters the employer of the unit and crew concerned shall negotiate a contract with the Contracting Officer on a time-charter, per diem basis. The employer must be a corporation or other legal intity acceptable to the Contracting Officer as a contracting party. Contracts will be subject to all terms and conditions required by the Contracting Officer for time-charter contracts, will be based upon the customary rate paid for such services and vessels in Korea as supported by a cost breakdown for the master, crew, vessel and administrative overhead not to exceed 25%, and shall recite payments in won. Contracts shall provide that no employee within the scope of the contract shall be deemed to be an employee of the United States or any of its agencies or instrumentalities for any purpose whatsoever. The execution, administration and continuance of the contract will be within the complete and sole discretion of the Contracting Officer.

0005

176

(4) When, as and if the unit and crew are nominated, tested, and accepted by this headquarters, and a contract is approved and executed the Japanese unit and crew to be replaced will be released subject to paramount requirements of efficient and uninterrupted operations.

c. Replacement of Japanese personnel by ROK technicians to supplement maritime activities ashore.

(1) This headquarters shall furnish the ROK Government a list of particular skills required, the number of persons essential to each skill, and the number of apprentices who may be attached to a particular operating unit.

(2) The ROK Government will nominate skilled individuals and those semi-skilled or otherwise qualified to absorb necessary training. All nominees shall be investigated, documented and tested for suitability by the ROK Government, or its agent. Nominees will be made available to representatives of this headquarters for test of qualifications or skills and may be rejected as lacking proper qualifications at the discretion of such representatives.

(3) Following acceptance of a nominee as a skilled technician or a qualified trainee, by this headquarters, he may be included among the employees in an appropriate contract operation such as vessel-hire, timecharter or ship repair. The contract for the operation will provide that all technicians and trainees are hired on a 90 day trial basis under supervision of representatives of this headquarters, who will assit in training of apprentices. Compensation of technicians and trainees shall be commensurate with customary wages paid in similar US Army job classifications in Korea. Ship's articles and articles of employment shall stipulate that no technician or trainee is an employee of the United States or any of its agencies or instrumentalities for any purpose whatsoever.

2. As an incident to acceptance of this replacement program, in the interest of a successful result, the ROK Government agrees to modify its present restricitive attitude to permit Japanese personnel in Korea to perform necessary functions ashore, pending their ultimate replacement.

3. The cooperation and participation of the ROK Government is considered to be indispensable to the success of this program. Recommendations and assistance of the ROK Government and its agencies are invited, purusant to the essential mutuality of effort.

4. Your acceptance of this program shall be indicated by your acknowledgement hereon.

EDWARD H. LASTAMO
Brigadier General, USA

0006

Suggestion by the Ministry of
Commerce and Industry.

20 Nov. 1953

1) The UN Forces in Korea shall pay the Korean power distributing companies (Seoul Electric Co. and South Korea Electric Co.) for electric services rendered (power distribution and construction), according to the duly established rate schedule, rules and regulations of these electric companies, as well as taxes in accordance with the ROK law.

2) The Korea Electric Power Co. shall pay the UN Forces in Korea for power delivered by the power barges under control of the UN Forces, at the wholesale rate duly prescribed by the ROK Government, deducting eight percent hadling expenses. Costs for materials, supplies or equipment, if any, financed with other funds than the UN Army funds, such as CRIK supply, furnished to the power barges, shall be deducted from the amount payable by the KEPCO.

3) The KEPCO shall pay the UN Forces for coal furnished to the Korean thermal plants by the UN Forces, at the coal sale price of the Korea Coal Corporation duly prescribed by the ROK Government.

4) The balance between the amount payable by the UN Forces to the Korean power distributing companies and the amount payable by the KEPCO to the UN Forces shall be paid by the UN Forces to a Korean Committee consisted of representatives of the Ministry of Commerce and Industry, KEPCO, SECO and SKECO. In case that the amount due from KEPCO exceeds that from the UN Forces, the KEPCO shall pay the balance to the UN Forces.

5) Old accounts shall be paid in suspence in a lump according to the amount and data submitted with guaranty by the UN Forces, KEPCO, SECO and SKECO; the final settlement shall be made after audit and adjustment, if necessary, by parties concerned during next three years.

6) New accounts shall be settled on the monthly pay basis in accordance with contracts to be entered into by the Ministry of Commerce and Industry, KEPCO, SECO and/or SKECO on the one hand and the UN Forces on the other.

174

0007

3 December 1953

Reference the informal electric power proposal, dated 20 November 1953, received from the Ministry of Commerce and Industry. Informal comments are listed categorically with reference to the 6 suggestions contained therein.

1. Reference is made to proposed electric power contractual drafts previously furnished at Seoul conferences on 31 August 1953, and 12 November 1953, and to letter, Commanding General, Korean Communications Zone, 15 September 1953, to Minister of Commerce and Industry, Republic of Korea. The two references state that the United States Army is to pay for electric services in accordance with the existing published rate schedules, rules, and regulations. Electric power contractual instruments state that Korean tax or duty is to be excluded from electric bills presented to the United States Army and is to be deducted if included in electric bills through error or otherwise.

2. The United States Army is interested in recovering only its out-of-pocket and plant rental costs for the power barges and its actual Tangin-Ri coal costs, as outlined in the references mentioned in the previous paragraph. The United States Army desires to use actual costs, not a prescribed wholesale rate. The United States Army does not propose to charge or to be charged any handling expenses. CRIK and similar type supplies are provided free to the Republic of Korea. Neither the United States Army nor the Republic of Korea is to charge or to be charged for any CRIK or similar type aid supplies.

3. The United States Army desires to recover only its actual out-of-pocket coal costs, not to use a prescribed wholesale rate.

4., 5., and 6. The methods for the payments of balances, between the Korean electric bills and the United States Army bills for electric power barges and Tagin-Ri coal costs, for both part and future bills were contained in the proposed contractual drafts presented on 12 November 1953, in Seoul. There is no objection to the Minister of Commerce and Industry being designated as the duly authorized representative of the Republic of Korea to sign the electric power contractual instruments.

0008

173

18 December 1953

Reference is made to informal comments on power account proposals dated 3 December 1953 and received via C. M. George 9 December 1953. Comments below correspond with similarly numbered paragraphs to referenced communication, and are forwarded with the approval of the Minister of Commerce and Industry.

1. Paragraph 1

a. Third Sentence: The distributions companies are obliged by law to collect the Electricity and Gas Tax (15%). The opinion of the Ministry of Finance heretofore has been that the Electricity and Gas Tas is applicable to charges for the service of electric power to the U.N. Forces (U.S. Army). This Ministry desires that electric power furnished to the U.N. Forces (U.S. Army) should not be taxed. It is currently conferring with the Ministry of Finance and recommending that the tax be held not applicable.

2. Paragraph 2.

a. First Sentence:

(1) Must the U.S. Army recover its "out-of-pocket and plant rental costs for the power barges and its actual Tangin-ri coal costs" in U.S. Dollars or ROK Hwan?

(2) If recovery by the U.S. Army is to be in ROK Hwan, conversion at what exchange rate is contemplated?

0009

172

b. Second Sentence: The necessity for the U.S. Army to recover actual costs rather than a prescribed wholesale rate is recognized and understood. This Ministry (KEPCO), on the other hand, cannot undertake to obligate the ROK Government for the unlimited reimbursement of U.S. Army-incurred power generation expenses over which this Ministry (KEPCO) can exercise no effective control.

c. Third Sentence:

(1) This Ministry (KEPCO) is required to credit to the foreign aid counterpart fund at the full prescribed wholesale rate (currently HW 1.56 per KWH) for all power received from the power barges. From this fund it was anticipated that KEPCO would be permitted to recover legitimate handling costs after deposits were made to the counterpart fund.

(2) With respect to power generated from domestic plants, the wholesale rate includes elements covering KEPCO's actual handling costs. All receipts and accounts payable from the sale to the distribution companies of power generated by the barges, however, is required to be deposited into, or earmarked for the foreign aid counterpart fund. KEPCO, thus, is prevented from recovering its costs of handling barge-gerated power unless it can recover its handling costs from the foreign aid counterpart fund in accordance with the principle governing the distribution of other aid commodities by ROK agencies.

(3) If the U.S Army cannot consider the problem of the KEPCO handling charge for barge-generated power, and instead desires to

0010

to supplant the counterpart fund formula with a direct contractual relationship to furnish supplemental electric power to the ROK at cost, it would appear equitable that this Ministry (KEPCO) should be relieved of further obligation to any foreign aid counterpart fund with respect to the proceeds from the sale of barge-generated power, and should be permitted to revise the wholesale rate to cover the pooled costs of all power generated, including both domestic and barge sources.

d/ Fourth Sentence: This sentence is understood to apply only with respect to the relationship between the U.S. Army and this Ministry (KEPCO) in the calculation of costs and offsetting credits.

3. Paragraph 3. The same general position applies as is indicated in par. 2 b above. This paragraph presents a further complication in that the Dae Han Coal Corporation is the sole official agency for the production, exportation, importation and distribution of all coal and coal products in Korea. Currently the Dae Han Coal Corporation has been authorized by the National Assembly action to furnish imported bituminious coal to domestic electric power gen ration plants at a price of HW 1800 per metric ton. This price, therefore, is required to be used in calculating the wholesale rate. This Ministry (KEPCO) is not authorized to purchase coal from any other source at any other price for this or any other purpose.

4. Paragraphs 4.5. and 6. No questions. 0011

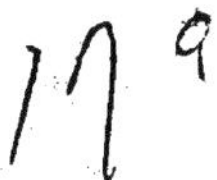

21 December 1953

Basis upon which Ministry of Commerce and Industry would like to resume discussion of power accounts:

Past Account:

1. KEPCO recognizes offset of approximately H₩ 604 million for Army expenses of power barges, less any amount which may be due to "proceeds from sale of aid goods" account (thru ROK Office of Supply) for CRIK-supplied POL, (unless it is determined (as by CEB action) that KEPCO is not liable to any counterpart fund).

2. KEPCO will pay for Army-supplied coal to Tangin-ri from a separately existing account, at the official ROK wholesale rate for electric power generation, of H₩ 1100 per metric ton. This account amounts to approximately H₩ 45 million.

3. Less actual costs to KEPCO of handling this power.

Future account:

1. Offset principle accepted with limitation that total of such costs to KEPCO shall not exceed total income to KEPCO from such operations.

0012

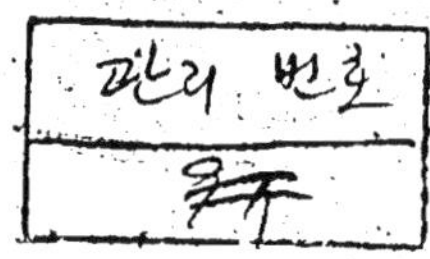

AGREEMENT BETWEEN THE REPUBLIC OF KOREA
AND THE UNITED STATES OF AMERICA REGARDING THE CUSTOMS
FUNCTIONS OF THE REPUBLIC OF KOREA
IN RELATION TO THE UNITED NATIONS FORCES

Whereas the United Nations, by the resolution of the Security Council of July 7, 1950, recommended all its Members providing military forces and other assistance to the Republic of Korea purusant to the resolutions of the Security Council of June 25 and 27, 1950, to make such forces and other assistance available to the Unified Command under the United States;

Whereas the Agreement on Economic Coordination between the Republic of Korea and the United States of America acting as the Unified Command, signed on May 24, 1952, declared, in its preamble, the concern on the part of the Unified Command to maintain a stable economy in the Republic of Korea and stipulated, in its article II, Paragraph 8, for the aforementioned Command to carry out its program of assistance to the Republic of Korea in such a way as to contribute to the stabilization of her economy;

Whereas the United Nations forces import into and export from the Republic of Korea a large amount of materials, supplies and equipment, consequence of which materially affects the conditions of economy in the Republic of Korea.

And whereas it is considered mutually desirable to conclude a provisional agreement between the Republic of Korea and the United States acting as the Unified Command regarding the former's customs functions in relation to the United Nations forces, pending a General Administrative agreement between such parties regarding problems arising from the disposition of such forces in the Republic of Korea;

Therefore, the Republic of Korea and the United States of America have entered into this Agreement in terms as set forth below:

ARTICLE I

In this Agreement the expression:

(a) "Parties to this Agreement" means the Government of the Republic of Korea, and the Government of the United States of America acting as the Unified Command.

(b) "United Nations forces" means those forces of the land, sea or air armed services of the States which are sent to Korea to engage in action pursuant to the United Nations Resolutions.

(c) "members of the United Nations forces" means personnel on active duty belonging to the United Nations forces when such persons are in Korea.

(d) "Civilian component" means the civilian persons of the nationality of any State sending forces to Korea pursuant to the United Nations Resolutions who are in the employ of the United Nations forces ~~when such persons~~ are in Korea, but excludes persons who are ordinarily resident in Korea.

(e) "Dependents" means the following persons, when such persons are in Korea:

(i) Spouse, and children under 21, of members of the United Nations, forces or of the civilian components;

(ii) Parents, and children over 21, of members of the United Nations forces or of the civilian components, if dependent for over half their support upon such members.

168

0013

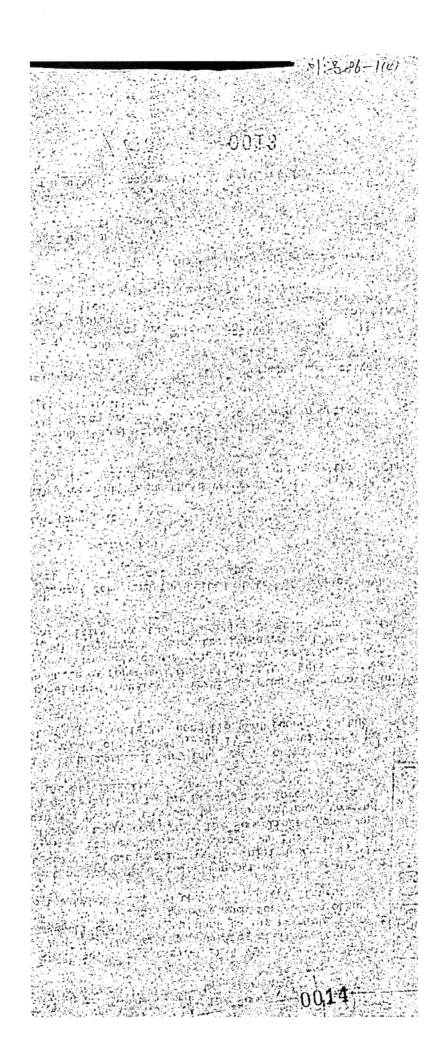

ARTICLE II

Save as provided to the contrary in this Agreement, members of the United Nations forces, the civilian component, and their dependents shall be subject to the laws and regulations administered by the customs authorities of Korea.

ARTICLE III

The United Nations forces or the non-appropriated fund organizations authorized and regulated by such forces including navy exchanges, post exchanges, messes, social clubs, theatres and newspapers may import free of duty all materials, supplies and equipment, exclusively for the fofficial use of the United Nations forces or for the use of the members of the United Nations forces, the civilian component, and their dependents. The duty-free importation shall be verified by a certificate issued by the United Nations forces authorities in a form agreed between Korea and the United Nations forces.

ARTICLE IV

Property consigned to and for the personal use of members of the United Nations forces, the civilian component, and their dependents, shall be subject to customs duties and all other duties that no duties shall be paid with respect to:

(a) Reasonable quantities of clothing and household goods of a type which would ordinarily be purchaed in their home States for everyday use for the private use of members of the United Nations forces, civilian component and their dependents, which are mailed into Korea through the United Nations military post offices.

ARTICLE V

Official documents under official seal and mail in the United Nations military postal channels shall not be subject to customs inspection.

ARTICLE VI

Goods which have been imported duty-free under Articles III and IV above:

(a) May be re-exported freely, provided that, in the Case of goods imported under Article III, a certificate is issued by the United Nations forces authorities in a form agreed between Korea and the United Nations forces.

(b) Shall not normally be disposed of in Korea by way of either sale or gift. However, in particular cases such disposal may be authorized on conditions agreed between the authorities of Korea and the United Nations forces.

ARTICLE VII

Exportation and re-importation of goods purchased in Korea shall be subject to the regulations in force in Korea. Such goods shall be regarded exported when deposited in a warehouse and deemed imported when removed from the warehouse.

ARTICLE VIII

In Articles III and IV of this Agreement, "duty" means customs duties and all other duties and taxes payable on importation or exportation, as the case may be, except dues and taxes which are no more than charges for services rendered.

1. The customs authorities of Korea shall have the right, when desirable,

0015

0016

in cooperation with the authorities of the United Nations forces to search members of the United Nations forces or civilian component and their dependents and examine their luggage and vehicles, and to seize articles pursuant to the laws and regulations administered by the customs authorities of Korea.

2. In order to prevent offences against customs and fiscal laws and regulations, the authorities of Korea and of the United Nations forces shall assist each other in the conduct of inquiries and the collection of evidence.

3. The authorities of the United Nations forces shall render all assistance within their power to ensure that articles liable to seizure by, or on behalf of, the customs or fiscal authorities of Korea are handed to those authorities.

4. The authorities of the United Nations forces shall render all assistance within their power to ensure apayment of duties, taxes and penalties payable by members of the United Nations forces or civilian component or their dependents.

ARTICLE X

The parties to this Agreement shall as promptly as possible take legislative, budgetafy and other measures necessary for the implementation of this Agreement.

ARTICLE XI

1. A Joint Board shall be established in Seoul as the means for consulation and agreement between the two Parties to this Agreement on Matters relating to the interpretation and implementation of this Agreement.

2. The Joint Board shall be composed of two representatives, one representing the Government of Korea and the other representing the United States of America, each of whom shall have one or more deputies and a staff. The Joint Board shall determine its own procedures, and arrange for such auxiliary organs and administrative services as may be required. The Joint Board shall be so organized that it may meet at any time at the request of either representative.

3. If the Joint Board is unable to reach agreement on any matter, it shall be settled through inter-governmental negotiations.

ARTICLE XII

This agreement shall enter into operation and effect immediately upon the signature hereof and shall continue in effect until it is mutually agreed that the need therefor has ceased. This Agreement and agreed revisions thereof shall terminate on the date by which all the United Nations Forces shall be withdrawn from Korea and shall resume its force automatically whenever such forces return to Korea.

IN WITNESS WHEREOF, the undersigned, being duly authorized by their respective Governments for the purpose, have signed this Agreement.

166

0017

0018

DONE at Seoul this   day of   1954 in the Korean and English languages, both texts being equally authoritative, in a single original which shall be deposited in the archives of the Government of Korea.

For the Government of the Republic of Korea

For the Government of the United States of America acting as the Unified Command:

165

0019

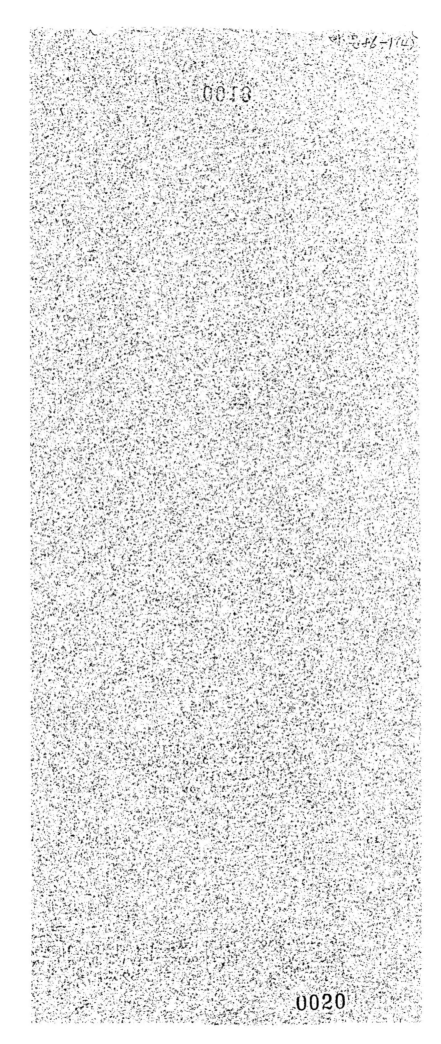

Ref: K-258/K-153 OFFICE OF THE PRIME MINISTER
REPUBLIC OF KOREA
C/o Seoul City Team APO 301 KCAC

Seoul, Korea
10 October 1953

To: CAIC/CS

SUBJECT: Duty free entry of non-minitary goods shipped to Korea via non-minitary transportation by or for UNC personnel, messes, etc.

1. I have, as requested in your DF of 28 September 1953, presented to the Ministry of Finance your letter requesting rescission or revision of the Customs Circular regarding the above question.

2. I have also discussed this matter at length with Mr. Kang Song Tae, Vice-minister of Finance and Mr. Park, the Acting Commissioner of Customs.

A formal reply will later be sent.

3. The following, however, represents the Ministry's attitude
(I) For funniture, crockery, glassware and other goods for Communal use (and not for re-sale) imported by Units, messes, clubs, etc. either dirctly or through private firms - such articles will be cleared free of duty provided the CO of the unit certifies to that effect and if that CO is of a rank less than full Colonel, the certification is countersigned by an Officer of the latter rank or above.
(II) As regards importation by UN personnel, the provision of Customs Circular 1498 must remain in force. That is that, without exception, the goods will be subject to the usual provision of the Customs Law and duty will be charged.

4. The Vice-minister does not wish in any way to inconvenience units, messes, etc., in obtaining their requirements duty free and has thus consented to your request as regards importation for such orgaizations. But he considers, and I think there is some justification in this, that to allow once again any UN employee or UNC officer or enlisted man to import goods for personal use free of duty would lead to a recrudescence of the serious abuses that existed hitherto. Even in your new forms figures could be altered and noughts added as was done in the past. The Vice-minister says that, after all, UN personner can import Via Army Post Offices from mail order houses or buy through PX's, goods sufficient for their normal use, free of duty.

0021

5. A conference of all Collectors of Customs is now proceeding and included on the agenda is this present question. Directions will be given to Collectors, before departure to their various ports, to implement this decision regarding communal-use goods.

6. If the promised official reply is not received shortly, please inform me and I will speak to the Minister again.

W.D. REEVE
CAAV-MF

c.c. to:

H.E. the Prime Minister
Vice-Minister of Finance
CAAD
CAPP
Agent General, UNKRA

0022

CAGG

Dear Sir:

The inclosed customs regulations, furnished by you through Mr. Reeve, concerning goods allegedly destined for UN Forces has been referred to General Herren for consideration. I have been instructed by him to inform you that your intended action is entirely in accord with our views.

Sincerely yours,

I Incl:
a/s

HOMER CASE
Brigadier General, USA
Commanding

Hon. Kang Song-T'ae
Chief of Customs Bureau
Ministry of Finance
Republic of Korea
Pusan, Korea

0023

CUSTOMS REGULATIONS

I. Goods now in stock, including goods shipped prior to 30 May and now en route to Korea against bona-fide orders accepted prior to April 30th.

a. Alcoholic and other beverages for official Locker Funds.

Will be cleared free of duty on presentation of a document signed by the authorized officer.

b. Alcoholic and other beverages ordered officially by a UNC Unit.

Will be cleared to UN units free of duty on presentation of a document signed by the CO and countersigned by CID MP.

c. Alcoholic and other beverages not covered in a. and b. above.

Will be cleared only on payment of full duties.

d. Goods other than alcoholic and other beverages (e.g.cameras, radios, luxury goods, etc.)

Will be subject to the usual provisions of the Customs Law and duty will be charged except that;

(i) If documents, satisfactory to the Customs, can be produced that an individual GI or officer had actually paid, before 30 April, for the article alleged to be imported for him and those documents are signed by the CO and counter-signed by CID - delivery free of duty will be allowed.

(ii) In order not to inconvenience units, messes, clubs, etc. which have ordered furniture, crockery, glass-ware and other goods for communal use through private firms - such articles will be cleared free of duty, provided the CO of the unit certifies to that effect.

0024

(II) FUTURE IMPORTATIONS - (i.e. GOODS NOT COVERED IN I ABOVE)

(a) Alcoholic and other beverages

Locker Funds only will be allowed to clear goods free of duty upon presentation of a document signed by an authorized officer (see I a. above). No alcoholic or other beverages will be delivered free of duty unless for an official Locker Funds.

(b) All goods other than included in (a). (e.g. radios and cameras etc.

will, without exception, be subject to the usual provisions of the Customs Law and duty will be charged.

0025

Ref: K-134

OFFICE OF THE ADVISER
Ministry of Finance

Pusan,
12 May 1953

To :CADC

SUBJECT: Goods, allegedly destined for UN Forces, imported by foreign firms.

1. I beg to acknowledge your D/F of May 1953 and have referred it to the Customs Commissioner.

2. We discussed the matter at length. The Commissione-r is most anxious not to inconvenience the supply of legitimate requirements, free of duty, to UN Units. On the other hand, he feels (Justifiably I think) that certain of the firms (and any innocent must suffer with the guilty) have for long been abusing their privileges, augmenting the already serious contraband traffic. They deserve no favourable consideration.

3. Subject to ratification by yourself and by the minister, Customs Bureau will lay down the following general principles:

(I) <u>GOODS NOW IN STOCK, INCLUDING GOODS SHIPPED PRIOR TO 30 April AND NOW IN ROUTE TO KOREA:</u>

(a) <u>Alcoholic and other beverages for official Locker Funds.</u>

Will be cleared free of duty on presentation of a document signed by the authorized officer.

(b) <u>Alcoholic and other beverages ordered officially by a UNC Unit.</u>

Will be cleared to Un Units free of duty on presentation of a document signed by the C.O. and counter-signed by C.I.D.of M.P.

(c) <u>Alcoholic and other beverages not covered in (a) and (b) above</u>

Will be cleared only on payment of full duties.

0026

(c) Goods other than alcoholic and other beverages. (e.g. cameras, radios, luxury goods etc.)

Will be subject to the usual provisions of the Customs Law and duty will be charged except that;

(i) If documents, satisfactory to the Customs, can be produced that an individual G.I. or officer had actually paid, before 30 April. for the article alleged to be imported for him and those documents are signed by the duty will be allowed.

(ii) In order not to inconvenience Units, Messes, Clubs, etc. which have ordered funiture, crockery, glassware and other goods for communal use through private firms-such articles will be cleared free of duty, provided the C.O. of the Unit certifies to that effect.

(II) FUTURE IMPORTATIONS - (i.e. GOODS SHIPPED AFTER I May 1953)

(a) Alcoholic and other beverages.

Locker Funds only will be allowed to clear goods free of duty upon presentation of a document signed by an authorized officer (see I (a) above). No alcoholic or other beverages will be delivered free of duty unless for an official Locker Funds.

(b) All goods other than included in (a). (e.g. radios and cameras etc)

Will, without exception, be subject to the usual provisions of the Customs law and duty will be charged.

4. I have suggested to the Customs Commissioner that if you concur, he notifies all firms concerned accordigly.

5. If agreed please confirm to me urgently. It is suggested all Commands be informed of the above procedures immediately.

(W.T. REEVE)
Adviser to the
Ministry of Finance

Copies to:-
CACK-EF
G-5 KCOMZ
Liaison Officer, Hq, KCOMZ
Customs Commissioner
U.S. Embassy (attention Financial Attache)
Mr. Prayad Buranasiri LOK
C.O. 2Ist CID, Pusan District,

0027

U.S. MPC in Korea Helping
To Feed Reds War Machine

Converted in Hongkong

By Robert Udick

Kyodo-UP

SEOUL, Apr. 13 --- Opium, gold and watches are being swapped for American military currency in Pusan's crocked alleys and black markets to feed the communist war machine.

Vicious Circle

It's a vicious circle. American soldiers trade their money for Korean currency with illegal money changers.

Merchant seamen at Pusan sell smuggled opium, gold and watches to Koreans for the clandestine U. S. money, much of which then goes to Hongkong's international money market.

In the next step, the U. S. Army believes, much of the currency winds up in Communist hands to build up Red might in the Far East.

Korea's sick economy, plus the closeness of China, makes Pusan the cheapest place in the world where the Communists can but American eash.

The U.S. money obtainable in Korea is Military Payment Certificates, a bread of currency few people in the United States have seen.

The Communists take a slight loss in Hongkong to convert blue-backed dollars into readily negotiable greenbacks, one of the most valuable currencies any world operator can carry in his pocket.

None of the transactions arelegal, since MPC's are sternly labeled "for use only in United States Military establishments by United States authorized personnel in accordance with appicable rules and regulations.

Obviously the rules do not include the Reds.

A qualified source said today MPC's are smuggled constantly from Pusan by Chinese crewmen arrive in Pusan the price of gold and watches on the black market drops 10 to 20 percent.

At the same time, MPC rates are hiked 10 to 20 percent.

"Military Payment Certificates can be purchased cheaper in Korea than anywhere in the Far East," one customs official said.

The blackmarket price today was just short of 300 whan per MPC dollar.

What becomes of the gold, watches and opium sold for illegally-obtained dollars?

The money changers hide most of the gold in their cellars against a rainy day. The watches go on the market.

Some of the opium finds Korea users and much of the rest is pushed into districts around army and air force installations to earn more MPC from soleier addicts as well as serving another Communist aim-undermining U.S. military strength in Korea.

164

0028

OFFICE OF THE PRIME MINISTER
REPUBLIC OF KOREA

0030

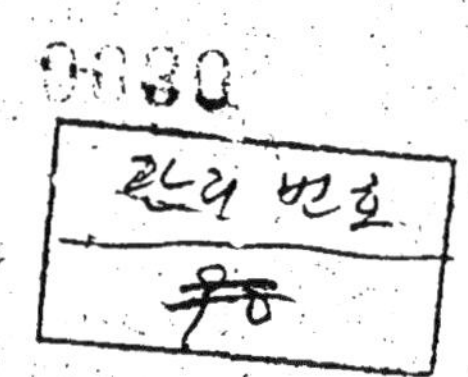

Seoul, Korea
26 April 1954

Dear General Taylor,

The lose of revenue to our Government through the illegal importation of goods into Korea is a metter of vital concern to our Government.

Most of the Japanese goods now in our markets are brought over by soldiers who go on Rest and Recuperation leave to Japan. Many of the Japanese goods on the Korean markets are brought in by the United Nations Forces personnel. It is generally known that the soldiers are selling items bought from the Post exchanges and the NAAFI stores to the local stores, for which they receive either objects of art, or in many cases Military Script with which to purchase goods in Japan. The soldier bringing in a considerable amount of items in his duffel bag, such as watches, pens, cameras, etc., is known to make a good profit from the transaction.

We also wish to bring to the attention of the military authorities the question of using the APO privilege by non-military personnel. At the ourbreak of the Korean War, we had no air and regular mail service, but how as they are fully established, this Government requests that the APO privilege be given only to military personnel, as our post office is in a position to take care of the mail.

As this Government is trying very hard to prevent smuggling by Korean civilians and Army personnel, we ask the United Nations Forces also to cooperate in eliminating smuggling both by soldiers returning from Japan and by non-military personnel through APO channels.

In as much as the correction of the abuses outlined above is to the mutual interest of our respective countries, and lies within your authority, we anticipate your full cooperation in initiating adequater corrective action.

In this connection I close, for your informations, a news article, "US MPC in Korea Helping To Feed Reds' War Machine" by Robert Udick as appeared in Asahi of April 13, 1954.

With highest esteam,

Yours very truly,

PAIK, TOO CHIN
Prime Minister
Republic of Korea

163

54-11-66

0029

0030

D R A F T

August 18, 1954

Sir,

I have the honour of writing to you concerning a conclusion of provisional Agreement regarding the functions of Korean customs' authorities with respect to the United Nations forces in Korea.

For some years, we have a serious problem of various luxury goods and other items that have been pouring into our country from abroad through some illegal means, and they are flooded throughout the country, thus creating one cause of greatly damaging effects to our economy. An effective measure to be agreed upon between the Korean Government and your Command to regulate lawful entry of goods from abroad will contribute, in no small way, toward the sound economy of Korea bosolutely desirable at this time of rehabilitation.

There exists, for some time, a strong opinion among the people and the Government circule that demands the desirability of concluding an Agreement defining the relationship between the Government of the Republic of Korea and the United Nations forces in regard to the former's customs' functions. Such an Agreement will remain in force pending conclusion of a general Administrative Agreement which shall cover other subjects also.

In the belief that a conclusion of the Agreement is in the mutual interests, I wish to propose formally, on behalf of the Korean Government, that negotiation be commenced between the representatives of my Government and the Unified Command. Upon the receipt of your consent, we shall appoint our representatives, and shall also suggest a date and place of the conference which will be mutually agreeable.

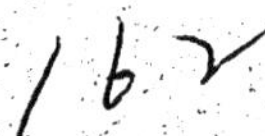

0031

Accept, Sir, the assurances of my highest consideration

Yung Tai Pyun
Minister of Foreign Affairs

General John E. Hull,
Commander-in-Chief,
United Nations Command,
APO 500

161

0032

DRAFT

I have the honor ofwriting to you concerning a conclusion of provisional Agreement regarding the functions of Korean customs' authorities with respect to the United Nations forces in Korea.

For some years, we have a serious problem of various luxury goods and other items that have been pouring into our country from abroad through some illegal means, and they are flooded throughout the country, thus creating one cause of greatly damaging effects to our economy. An effective measure to be agreed upon between the Korean Government and the United Nations Command to regulate lawful entry of goods from abroad will contribute,in no small way, toward the sound economy of Korea absolutely desirable at this time of rehabilitation.

There exists, for some time, a strong opinion among the people and the Government circule that demands the desirability of concluding an Agreement defining the relationship between the Government of the Republic of Korea and the United Nations forces in regard to the former's Customs' functions. Such an Agreement will remain in force pending conclusion of a General Administrative Agreement which shall cover other subjects also.

In the belief that a conclusion of the Agreement is in the mutual interests, I wish to propose formally, on behalf of the Korean Government, that negotiation be commenced between the representatives of my Government and the Unified Command. Upon the receipt of your consent, we shall appoint our representatives, and shall also suggest a date and place of the conference which will be mutually agreeable.

Accept, my dear Ambassador, the assurances of my highest consideration.

Yung Tai Pyun
Minister of Foreign Affairs

His Excellency
Ellis O. Briggs,
Ambassador of the United States
Seoul

0033

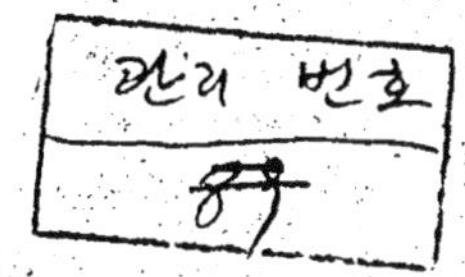

My dear Ambassador:

I have the honour of writing to you concerning a conclusion of provisional Agreement regarding the functions of Korean customs' authorities with respect to the United Nations forces in Korea.

For some years, we have a serious problem of various luxury goods and other items that have been pouring into our country from abroad through some illegal means, and they are flooded throughout the country, thus creating one cause of greatly damaging effects to our economy. An effective measure to be agreed upon between the Korean Government and the United Nations Command to regulate lawful entry of goods from abroad will contribute, in no small way, toward the sound economy of Korea absolutely desirable at this time of rehabilitation.

There exists, for some time, a strong opinion among the people and the Government circlnding an Agreement defining the relationship between the Government of the Republic of Korea and the United Nations forces in regard to the formcr8s customs' functions. Such an Agreement will remain in force pending conclusion of a General Administrative Agreement which shall cover other subjects also.

In the belief that a conclusion of the Agreement is in the mutual interests, I wish to propose formally, on behalf of the Korean Government, that negotiation be commenced between the representatives of my Government and the Unified Command. Upon the receipt of your consent, we shall appoint our representatives, and shall also suggest a date and place of the conference which will be mutually agreeable.

0035

Accept, My dear Ambassador, the assurances of my highest consideration.

C. W. Cho
Acting Minister

His Excellency
Ellis O. Briggs
Ambassador of the United States
Seoul

158

0036

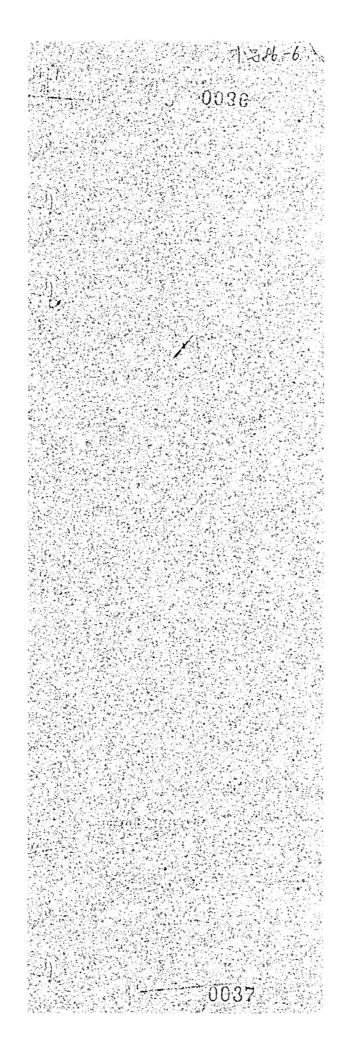

촬영 X

American Embassy
Seoul, Korea,
January 27, 1955

관리번호
58

My dear Dr. Pyun:

검토필(1964.12.30.)

On December 6, 1954, the Embassy received a letter from the Acting Minister of Foreign Affairs, dated December 2, 1954, concerning the possibility of negotiating an agreement with the United States defining the relationship between the Government of the Republic of Korea and the United Nations forces in regard to the former's customs functions. The Acting Minister enclosed a draft to form a basis of possible discussions.

This matter was already under study at General Hull's headquarters when the Acting Minister's letter was received atthe Embassy. I am advised that General Hull informed you in a letter dated December 3, 1954, that he had directed that the entire matter be studied with a view to promulgating uniform procedures which will provide the Korean Customs officials an improved and reasonable opportunity to exercise their responsibility. I am pleased to be able to inform you that you will receive copies of the regulations covering these new procedures in the near future. I hope that you will find that they meet the requirements of the Government of the Republic of Korea without the necessity of negotiating a formal agreement, particularly since it will be possible to put them in effect as soon as they are completed.

I am, my dear Mr. Minister,

Sincerely yours,

Ellis O. Briggs
American Ambassador

His Excellency
Pyun Yung-tai,
Minister of Foreign Affairs of
the Republic of Korea.

157

0038

0038

0039

American Embassy,
Seoul, Korea,
January 27, 1955

관리번호
58

My dear Dr. Pyun:

검토필(1966.12.30.)

On December 6, 1954, the Embassy received a letter from Acting Minister of Foreign Affairs, dated December 2, 1954, concerning the possibility of negotiating an agreement with the United States defining the relationship between the Government of the Republic of Korea and the United Nations forces in regard to the former's customs functions. The Acting Minister enclosed a draft to form a basis of possible discussions.

This matter was already under study at General Hull's headquarters when the Acting Minister's letter was received at the Embassy. I am advised that General Hull informed you in a letter dated December 3, 1954, that he had directed that the entire matter be studied with a view to promulgating uniform procedures which will provide the Korean Customs officials an improved and reasonable opportunity to exercise their responsibility. I am pleased to be able to inform you that you will receive copies of the regulations covering these new procedures in the near future. I hope that you will find that they meet the requirements of the Government of the Republic of Korea without the necessity of negotiating a formal agreement, particularly since it will be possible to put them in effect as soon as they are completed.

I am, my dear Mr. Minister,

Sincerely yours,

검토필(1965.6.30.)

Ellis O. Briggs
American Ambassador

His Excellency
Pyun Yung-tai,
Minister of Foreign Affairs of
the Republic of Korea.

157

0040

April 28, 1955

관리번호 87

Dear Mr. Charge d'Affaires:

검토필(196 .12.30.)

I have the honour to initiate a proposal to conclude an Administrative Agreement between the Government of the Republic of Korea and the Government of the United States of America, and enclose herewith a draft of the Agreement. With regard to this proposal, I would like first to refer to my note dated December 2, 1954, concerning a conclusion of provisional Agreement regarding the functions of Korean customs authorities with respect to the United Nations forces in Korea. Particular reference was made in the note to the effect that such customs agreement will remain in force pending conclusion of a General Administrative Agreement which shall cover other subjects also.

Having in mind that the United Nations forces under the Unified Command are and will be disposed in and about the territory of the Republic of Korea until the objective of the United Nations in Korea will have been achieved pursuant to the resolutions of the United Nations Security Council of June 25, 1950, June 27, 1950 and July 7, 1950, it is the belief of the Korean Government that terms shall be provided, for the interests of both parties, to govern the disposition of and render convenience to the said forces in and about Korea, and that they shall be determined through mutual agreement between the Republic of Korea and the United States of America acting as the Unfied Command in accordance with "The Resolution on the Settlement of the Unified Command" of the Security Council of the United Nations of July 7, 1950. A practical and effective Administrative Agreement to be concluded between the said two parties will help minimize misunderstanding and maximize cooperativeness between the Korean people and United Nations forces personnel in Korea.

The Honourable Carl W. Strom,
Charge d'Affaires,
Embassy of the United States of America
Seoul, Korea

156

0041

In the belief that a conclusion of the Agreement is in the mutual interests, I wish to propose formally, on behalf of the Government of the Republic of Korea, that negotiation will be commenced between the representatives of Korean Government and the United States Government. Upon the receipt of your consent, we will proceed to decide the date and place of the conference, which will be mutually agreeable.

Accept, dear Mr. Charge d'Affaires, the assurances of my highest consideration.

Enclosure: Draft of Administrative Agreement

Y. T. Pyun
Minister

155

0042

American Embassy,
Seoul, Korea,
May 9, 1955

관리번호
86.

My dear Mr. Minister:

I have the honor to acknowledge the receipt of your letter of April 28, 1955, enclosing a Draft of an Administrative Agreement Between the Republic of Korea and the Unified Command regarding the Status of the United Nations Forces.

I note that you request that negotiations be commenced between representatives of the Governments of the United States and of the Republic of Korea looking toward the completion of an agreement.

I have transmitted a copy of the Ministry's Draft to the Department's instructions. I shall be pleased to advise you as soon as these are received and shall look forward to a happy outcome of our negotiations.

Acceot, Mr. Minister, the assurances of my highest condideration.

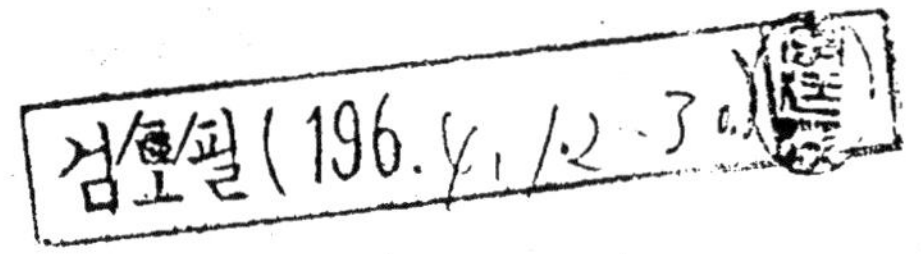

His Excellency
Pyun, Yung-tai,
Minister of Foreign Affairs,
Republic of Korea

154

0043

HEADQUARTERS
FAR EAST COMMAND
APO 500

AGJ 000.5 EJ/C 14 May 1955

SUBJECT: Controls Concerning Property Brought into Korea by Individuals

TO: Commanding General, United States Army Forces, Far East and Eighth United States Army, APO 343
Commander Naval Forces, Far East, c/o FPO San Francisco, California
Commander, Far East Air Forces, APO 925

1. Rescission: Letter, AGJ 000.5 EJ/C, Hq Far East Command, 6 December 1954, subject: "Establishment of Enforcement Procedure to Detect Smuggling in Korea."

2. Individuals, subject to the military jurisdiction of a force which has been sent by any State pursuant to Security Council and General Assembly resolutions which called upon all States to lend every assistance to the United Nations action in Korea, shall be permitted to bring into Korea, free from customs duties and other such charges, only reasonable quantities of privately owned property for personal or family use; provided that the possession or entry into Korea of such property does not otherwise violate force, service or command regulations.

3. These instructions implement the policy stated above by establishing procedures with respect to property brought into Korea by individuals entering the country, where the entry of the individual and his accompanying baggage is by means of United States military transportation. The procedures will come into force and effect forty-five days following the publication date of this letter.

a. The Commander, Far East Air Forces, shall assume responsibility for the enforcement of the procedures at ports of entry under the jurisdiction of the Far East Air Forces.

b. The Commanding General, United States Army Forces, Far East and Eighth United States Army, shall assume responsibility for the enforcement of the procedures at other United States areas and facilities.

c. The Commanding General, United States army Forces, Far East and Eighth United States Army, is assigned responsibility for printing and distributing suppiies of the declaration form provided for hereinbelow (Inclosure 1). Consideration should be given to making the forms

153

0044

b. This declaration form, Inclosure 1, shall be used to describe the privately owned property being brought into Korea by the declarant (property carried in by the individual, hold or other baggage arriving with the individual, and other property held at the port awaiting the arrival of the individual). Military equipment and supplies which have been issued to or purchased by a declarant will not be listed or described in the declaration form. Reasonable quantities of privately owned personal effects, owned by and being brought into Korea for the personal use of the declarant, or for the use of a member of the family of the person making the declaration, may be described as "personal effects and clothing," without further detailed description, except that all items of property identified by serial numbers (expensive cameras, etc.) must be itemized and described separately.

c. Upon receipt, port authorities shall take the following actions concerning the declarant, the declaration form, and the property of each individual at the port of entry:

(1) United States forces authorities will review forms presented by individuals subject to United States courts-martial jurisdiction, and conduct spot checks or examinations of hand carried and other baggage or property at the port, noting on the declaration forms, that such spot checks or examinations have been accomplished. The examination may be similar to checks or inspections conducted by customs authorities. One copy of the noted form shall be (returned to the declarant. One copy of the noted form shall be) forwarded immediately to the nearest customs office of the Korean Government. In the event a spot check or examination results in the location of contraband property or items in excess of usual requirements, contraband and items identified as in excess of usual requirements shall be segregated from the other property of the individual concerned. Disposition of the property so segregated, and actions taken with respect to an individual who has attempted to bring into Korea the segregated items, shall be purusant to applicable service or command regulations. Where segregated property has been or is to be disposed of pursuant to applicable service or command regulations, the copy of the declaration form forwarded to the Korean Customs office shall include remarks as to the property segregated and as to its disposition or pending disposition.

(2) When persons, identified in paragraph 4a(1), above, not subject to United States courts-martial jurisdiction, arrive in Korea, United States forces authorities shall channel such persons and the declaration forms presented by them to the representative at the port of the force which has jurisdiction over such individuals. As requested, United States forces authorities shall assist this force representative, in actions taken by the representative similar to tho spot checks or

0045

examinations discussed above. If there is no representative, at the port of the force which has jurisdiction over an individual:

(a) Local United States military authorities may act for such force in the spot check or examination at the request of appropriate authorities of the concerned force.

(b) The individual and his property and baggage may be provided transportation to the nearest unit of the force to the port, for spot check or examination by competent officials of the force.

(c) As requested by the appropriate authorities of the concerned force, the spot check orexamination may be deferred until the arrival at the port of entry of a force representative.

6. Persons identified in paragraph 4a(a) above will not be required to complete or submit Inclosure 1, except at the direction of the officer in charge of the unit.

7. When persons identified in paragraph 4b above enter Korea through ports of entry or facilities operated or controlled by the United States forces, it shall be the responsibility of the United States military authorities of the converned port of entry or facility to turn over such individuals and their property and baggage to the nearest Korean Government customs office immediately following the debarkation of the individual from the aircraft or vessel.

8. When persons identified in paragraph 4c above enter Korea through ports of entry or facilities operated or controlled by the United States forces, such persons shall be placed in touch with representatives of an appropriate agency or government in Korea, and actions with respect to clearing such personnel and their property and baggage into Korea through Korean Customs shall be the responsibility of such representatives.

9. The procedures stated above do not limit or restrict usual law enforcement activities, or additional measures taken separately or in cooperation with Korean officials designed to prevent or detect smuggling or the introduction of contraband property into Korea.

BY COMMAND OF GENERAL TAYLOR:

G. W. NELSON
Colonel, AGC
Adjutant General

1 Incl
Declaration Form

151

0046

June 13, 1955

관리번호
83

Dear General Lemnitzer:-

I have the honour to acknowledge the receipt of the letter of May 14, 1955 signed by General Maxwell D. Taylor, the then-Commander in Chief of the United Nations Command enclosing a copy of the letter AgJ 000.5 EJ/C signed by Colonel C.W. Nelson of the Headquarters of the same Command, the subject of which reads "Controls concerning Property Brought into Korea by Individuals."

The Ministry has taken note of the procedures described in the enclosed letter signed by Colonel Nelson.

While appreciating the voluntary cooperation on the part of the Command with respect to customs fundtions of the Republic of Korea, I wish to inform you of the desire of the Korean Government to commence negotiation with the Government of the United States, as soon as possible, for the conclusion of a comprehensive agreement between the Republic of Korea and the Unified Command regarding the status of the United Nations forces in Korea, etc., which will also define the customs functions of the Korean Government, as laready proposed in my letter of April 25, 1955 addressed to Mr. Carl W. Strom, Charge D'Affaris of the Embassy of the United States in Seoul, to which you can easily refer, if you think it advisable.

검토필(196.Y.12.30.)

Y. T. Pynn
Minister of Foreign Affairs

General Lyman L. Lemnitzer
Commander-in- Chief
United Nations Command,
Tokyo, Japan

0047

150

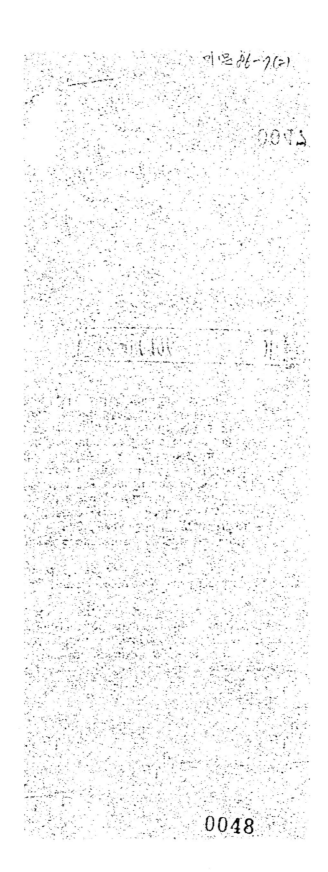

26 July 1955

Dear Minister Pyun:

Thank you very much for your letter of 13 June 1955, in which you acknowledge receipt of General Taylor's letter of 14 May 1955, with the inclosures pertaining to customs functions of the Republic of Korea.

I have noted the desire of the Korean Government to commence negotiations with the Government of the United States for a Status of Forces Agreement between the Korean Government and the Unified Command. This matter is presently under study by the Departmet of my government in Washington.

Current thinking on this matter is that it would be preferable that negotiations now in progress or pending be completed before the initiation of negotiaions for an agreement of the type in question. Ambassador Lacy advises me that a proposed treaty of friendship, commerce and navigation between our respective governments is under consideration, as well as an agreement guaranteeing investments, and that he is anxious to complete these matters before taking up any other major negotiations.

I am sure you are also aware that the Unified Command cannot participate in a negotiation of any Status of Force Agreement without the prior consent of our allies within the United Nations Command. It is anticipated that the task of obtaining this consent will be difficult and time consuming.

Sincerely,

L. L. Lemnitzer
General, United States Army
Commander-in-Chief

His Excellency Pyun Yung-Tai
Minister of Foreign Affairs of
The Republic of Korea

0049

14P

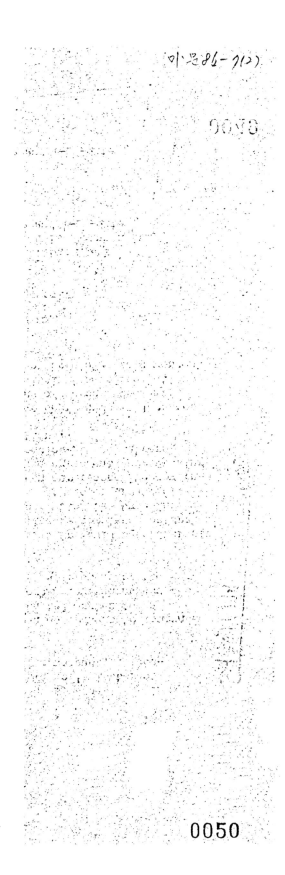

July 28, 1955

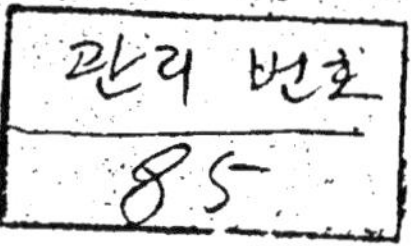

My Dear General,

Let me acknowledge with thanks the receipt of your good letter of July 26, 1955 regarding the negotiation of an administrative agreement between the Unified Command and this Government. An agreement of this nature has been long due and your note of concurrence in the wish of concluding one is most welcome and heartening.

Since the Unified Command is reposed in the American hands nad since the American forces form the predominant components of the United Nations forces, we need not envisage real difficulties in securing consent of other allies in the matter.

As regards the treaty of freindship, commerce and navigation it is near completion, awaiting to be finalized very soon, and the agreement guaranteeing investments, already in complete draft form, will not consume much time in negotiation.

This Government is very desirous of starting the negotiation for an administrative agreement immediately after the two aforementioned treaties are concluded. Our allies, too, fully aware 9f the need pf such an agreement, will not, Iam sure, make difficulties about starting preliminary negotiationfor it similtaneously with the Unified Command seeking to obtain their consent as to the matter.

Thankng you once again for the long awaitied offer,

Yours sincerely,

검토필(196. . 12. 30 .)

Y. T. Pyun
Minister of Foreign Affairs

General L. L. Lemnitzer
Commander-in-Chief
United Nations Command

0051

148

□ 조 외무부장관의 Dowling 주한미대사와 한·미간 주둔군지위협정 교섭 개시를 재촉구 [illegible] (57.1.5 회견)

January 5, 1957

관리번호 82

Excellency:

I have the honour to refer to the Foreign Minister's note addressed to Mr. Carl W. Strom, Charge d'Affairs ad interim of the Embassy of the United States of America in Korea dated April 28, 1955 enclosing a draft of an Administrative Agreement between the Republic of Korea and the Unified Command for establishment of the Status of the United Nations Forces in Korea.

In the afore-said note, the Minister informed the Government of the United States of America of the desire of the Korean Government to commence negotiations with the United States Government for the said Status of Forces Agreement which will also define the forer's customs functions as referred to in my letter of December 2, 1954.

To this proposal, however, no acceptance has been given as yet, although the American Charge d'Affairs notified in his replying note of May 9, 1955, that upon obtaining his Government's view on the said request, he would communicate with the Minister.

His Excellency
The right honorrable
Walter C. Dowling
Ambassador of the United Statex of
America to the Republic of Korea
Seoul, Korea

검토필(196.4.12.31.)

147

0052-1

(28)E
57-3-1

외-3-1 (2) 미오86-9(6)

0053

I hereby wish again to propose, on behalf of my Government, that negotiation be commenced at an earliest possible date between the representatives of the Korean Government and the United States Government. In connection with this re-proposal, I would like further to refer to the note of July 26, 1955 addressed to the Foreign Minister by General Lemnitzer advising on this matter, a copy of which is enclosed herewith for information.

General Lemnitzer expressed his views on the possibility of negotiating the said agreement in the above note to the effect that the United States Government envisages difficulties in commencing immediately negotiations for a proposed agreement for the following two reasons:

The one reason was that it would be preferable to the American Government that negotiations for a proposed treaty of Friendship, Commerce and Navigation between the two countries as well as an agreement guaranteeing investment be completed before the initiation of negotiation for an agreement in question. The other was that the Unified Command cannot participate in negotiation of such agreement without the prior consent of Allies within the Unified Command and it is anticipated that the task of obtaining such consent will be difficult.

Attention, however, is paid to the fadt that points indicated above constitute no longer difficulties about negotiating the said

마-문 86-8

- 3 -

0055

0024

agreement under the present circumstances

Negotiation for a proposed treaty of Freidnship, Commerce and Navigation has been completed and the treaty is now waiting to be formally signed. As regards the agreement guaranteeing investments, discussions have been completed on provisions of its draft and now the work of finalizing it remains only. Under Nations Forces, there exist no difficulties, it is believed, in securing consent of other allies as to the matter.

And thus, in case such consent has not been obtained as yet, it is, therefore, proposed that preliminary negotiations be started first between both representatives of the Korean Government and the United States Government, since it is considered that negotiations with other allies can be carried on seperately in accordance with terms agreed upon between the two countries above.

It is sincerely requested that the concurrence of the United States Government be given to the wish of the Korean Government to have negotiation for the agreement.

Please accept, Excellency, the renewed assurances of my highest consideration.

Chung W. Cho
Acting Minister
of Foreign Affairs

57-3-3

Enclosure: A copy of General Lemnitzer's Letter dated July 26, 1955.

145

0056

57-3-1 (2)

0028

0057

2. 주둔군지위 ~~SOFA~~ 협정 관련 1.15자 조외무부장관 서한에 대한 ~~교섭 개시 요구에 대한~~

주한미 Dowling 대사의 회한 (57.1.15)

American Embassy,
Seoul, Korea,
January 15, 1957

Excellency:

I have the honor to acknowledge the receipt of your note of January 5, 1957, proposing that negotiations be commenced at the earliest possible date between the representatives of the Republic of Korea and of the United States of America, in respect to an Administrative Agreement between the Republic of Korea and the Unified Command for Establishment of the Status of the United Nations Forces in Korea as proposed by the Government of the Republic of Korea in a draft transmitted on April 28, 1955.

I have transmitted a copy of your note to my Government, and have requested its instructions. I shall look forward to further consultation with you as soon as these instructions have been received.

Please accept, Excellency, the renewed assurances of my highest consideration.

His Excellency
Cho Chung-hwan,
Minister for Foreign Affairs,
Republic of Korea,
Seoul

0058-1

144

57-3-4

57-3-2 (1)　　미.문86-8

0053

3. 주미대사관의 미국무성 SOFA 협정개시 촉구 교섭 보고 (57.2.4)

(주둔군지위) 교섭 방침관련 접촉 결과 보고

February 4, 1957

MEMORANDUM TO: Minister Han

SUBJECT: Administrative Agreement

FROM: First Secretary Han

I had a conference this morning on the above subject with Mr. David Nes, Chief of Korea Desk of the State Department. As you know, our Government wants to commence negotiations on this subject and has instructed this Embassy to expedite the matter at this end.

Mr. Nes said that only a few days ago the State Department received a dispatch from its Embassy in Seoul enclosing the latest letter (dated January 5, 1957) from Foreign Minister Cho to Ambassador Dowling. He said that inasmuch as this problem involves the Defense Department and legal authorities, the State Department cannot decide alone what to do and will have to have inter-departmental conferences before a dedision can be reached. He estimated that four to six weeks would be required for this purpose. He promised to work on it actively and said he will let us know as soon as his government decides what to do. At the same time, he said, a detailed reply will be sent to Foreign Minister Cho through the Embassy in Seoul.

Commenting on the difficulty of starting negotiations on this matter, Mr. Nes said that legally Korea is still in a state of war and that it would be difficult for the United States to negotiate an administrative agreement such as that exists with NATO countries or with Japan. He mentioned that in the Treaty with NATO countries, there is a provision that provides for instant termination of the Treaty in case of a war.

I said that this matter of Administrative Agreement was first taken up by our government in April, 1955, at which time we presented to the American Embassy in Seoul a draft of the Agreement for its study. I said that although there were several exchanges of communications with the Embassy in Seoul and also with Gen. Lemnitzer after that, no definite reply has yet been given by the U.S. government. I said that according to General Lemnitzer's letter to our Foreign Minister dated July 26, 1955, there were two

143

0060-1 57-3-5

57 - 3 - 3 (2) 0080

reasons why negotiations could not be started. First, the U.S. government preferred to start negotiations after the Treaty of Friendship, Commerce and Navigation had been signed. Second, the United States had to get prior consent of the countries whose forces are in the United Nations Forces. The first reason, I said, no longer exists. As for the second reason, I said it should not be tooddifficult if our two governments started negotiations first and then arrived at a conclusion as to the draft of the Agreement, and then got the Allies concerned to agree to it or negotiate on it. Whatever we do, I said, something should be done to get the ball rolling.

Mr. Nes replied that although Gen. Lemnitzer gave those two reasons, he, or rather, the State Department dees not think that they constituted the major difficulties. The State Department blieves, he said, that the major difficulty lies in that Korea is still legally in a state of war. Anyway, he said, no definite answer could be given unless some conclusions were reached at inter-departmental conferences, after which both our Foreign Minister and this Embassy would be notified in detail as to what the American position is on the matter.

57-3-3(2) 미문86-8(6)

0063

COPY

June 29, 1957

My dear Mr. Ambassador:

I have the honor to remind your Government, as I have orally mentioned to you on several occasions, that the conclusion of an Administrative Agreement defining and setting forth in detail the status of United States troops stationed in Korea is still pending.

On April 25, 1955, our draft proposal of an Administrative Agreement between this Government and the Unified Command, to establish the status of United Nations forces in Korea, was addressed to your Embassy. On November 1, 1956, it was proposed that a separate agreement be negotiated between representatives of this Government and the United States Government, in case of difficulty in obtaining early consent of the other Allied Governments.

In the absence of such an administrative agreement, a temporary agreement was made through the exchange of Notes at Taejon, on July 12, 1950, concerning the exclusive jurisdiction by court-martial of the United States over members of the United States Military Establishment in Korea. This agreement, which is still in force, was improvised to meet an emergency situation and is not considered sufficient to meet effectively all the

/complex

His Excellency
Ambassador Walter Dowling,
American Embassy,
Seoul.

0064

57-3-17

57 - 3 - 4 (2)

마문84-26(2)

0065

complex and complicated problems arising from the presence of United States troops in Korea.

This Government is strongly convinced that the early conclusion of a formal and detailed agreement on the status of United States troops in Korea would serve to strengthen cordial relations between our people and American military personnel, and would provide great satisfaction to the mutual cause and interest of both countries.

I wish to state again that this Government is most desirous of receiving the concurrence of the United States Government in order to commence negotiations for an administrative agreement along the lines of the proposal of April, 1955. Your Government's earliest favorable consideration of this matter is most sincerely desired.

Accept, Excellency, renewed assurances of my highest consideration.

Chung W. Cho
Minister

0066 57-3-8

57-3-4(2)

미.문84-26(2)

0067

(사본)

September 10, 1957

SUBJECT: Proposed Agreement on the Status of United Nations or United States Forces in Korea

The Government of the Republic of Korea, keenly desiring to conclude an agreement which would define the status of the United Nations armed forces in Korea, with the Government of the United States of America acting for the Unified Command in accordance with "The Resolution on the Settlement of the Unified Command" of the Security Council of the United Nations of July 7, 1950, initially proposed to the Government of the United States of America through the Foreign Minister's note of April 28, 1955, attached hereto as Annex A, that negotiations should be opened for that purpose.

It is also recalled that, as there was no positive reaction on the part of the United States Government on the said matter, the Korean Government again renewed its proposal to the United States through the Foreign Minister's notes of January 5, 1957 and June 29, 1957 respectively, copies of which are attached hereto as Annex B and Annex C. No definite reply stating the position of the United States Government in regard to these proposals has been received as yet.

Attention is invited to the note (Annex D hereto) of General Lemnitzer of July 26, 1955 addressed to the Foreign Minister, in which the former, in expressing his views on the possibility of negotiations on the said Agreement, stated that the United States Government envisages difficulties in commencing negotiations immediately for two reasons:

1) It would be preferred by the United States Government that the negotiations for the proposed treaty of Friendship, Commerce and Navigation between the two countries as well as

/an agreement

0068

~~54~~ 57-3-10

57 - 3 - 6 (11)

미·운 80-1(11)

0069

an agreement guaranteeing investments be completed before the initiation of negotiations for the agreement in question;

2) The Unified Command could not participate in negotiations of such an agreement without the prior consent of the allies within the Unified Command, and the task of obtaining such consent is time consuming.

As for the first reason mentioned above, the Korea-United States Treaty of Friendship, Commerce and Navigation has been already signed and is now only awaiting exchange of the instruments of ratification. As for the agreement guaranteeing investment, i.e. the so-called MSA Guarantee Agreement proposed by the United States Government, the Korean Government is preparing the final draft, and a definite agreement should be reached in the immediate future.

As for the second reason, the Government of the Republic of Korea is of the opinion that, as the United States forces in Korea actually constitute the preponderant components of the United Nations Forces under the Unified Command, the negotiations could be commenced first between the Korean Government and the United States Government regarding the status of the United States forces in Korea.

Apart from the above-mentioned two reasons, it is presumed that the reluctance on the part of the United States Government to commence negotiations on this subject is based on the fact that Korea is technically still in a state of war. Needless to say, however, active hostilities ceased in 1953, and the danger of a recurrence of hostilities is not considered imminent. It cannot be predicted how long the current situation will last.

Under these circumstances, it is not realistic to consider the current situation, which has lasted so long, a state of war in a

/virtual sense.

0070 ~~55~~ 57-3-11

57-3-6 마름90-1

0071

virtual sense. Therefore, the Korean Government does not consider that anything in the current situation in Korea prevents the Governments of the Republic of Korea and the United States of America from entering into the relations which would be established if the Agreement under reference be concluded. As for the anxiety concerning the possible recurrence of hostilities in Korea, there would be no reason why the parties to the proposed Agreement should not review the applicability of the provisions concerned in such case.

What the Korean Government desires to conclude with the United States is nothing but such agreements similar to those concluded by the latter with NATO powers in 1951 and with Japan in 1952 on the same subject.

In the absence of such an agreement between the Republic of Korea and the United States of America, and in view of the then-prevailing conditions of warfare and urgent necessity, a modus vivendi, which partly defined the status of the United States forces in Korea, came into being between the two governments through the exchange of notes at Taejon on July 12, 1950 concerning the exclusive jurisdiction by court-martial of the United States over its military personnel in Korea. In view of the changed conditions after the summer of 1953, the aforesaid provisional arrangement of 1950 is no longer appropriate in its nature nor sufficient to meet and solve adequately, under the circumstances, all of the complicated problems and matters arising daily because of the stationing and disposition of United States forces in Korea.

In this connection, it is with regret that numerous incidents must be mentioned which occurred between the United States army personnel and local civilians; in most cases, incidents caused by delinquency on the part of members of the United States forces in

/Korea,

56 0072 57-3-12

57 -3-6

마.음80-1

0073

Korea, involving many casualties and much damage to valuable property. All of such incidents, according to the provisional arrangement of 1950, are exclusively within the jurisdiction of the United States. The Korean Government especially fears that such incidents, and the present way of application of justice, may injure the friendly relationship existing between the peoples of the two countries.

The Government of the Republic of Korea again requests the Government of the United States of America to give favorable consideration to the proposal of the Korean Government so that negotiations between the two governments may be commenced as early as possible. A prompt conclusion of the Agreement in question would undoubtedly serve to promote increased friendship between the peoples of the two countries.

57 -3-6 미·북PO-1

0075

ANNEX A.

韓.UN軍關係 (出入國, 關稅의 措置)

April 28, 1955

Dear Mr. Chargé d'Affaires:

I have the honour to initiate a proposal to conclude an Administrative Agreement between the Government of the Republic of Korea and the Government of the United States of America, and enclose herewith a draft of the Agreement. With regard to this proposal, I would like first to refer to my note dated December 2, 1954, concerning a conclusion of provisional Agreement regarding the functions of Korean customs authorities with respect to the United Nations forces in Korea. Particular reference was made in the note to the effect that such customs agreement will remain in force pending conclusion of a General Administrative Agreement which shall cover other subjects also.

Having in mind that the United Nations forces under the Unified Command are and will be disposed in and about the territory of the Republic of Korea until the objective of the United Nations in Korea will have been achieved pursuant to the resolutions of the United Nations Security Council of June 25, 1950, June 27, 1950 and July 7, 1950, it is the belief of the Korean Government that terms shall be provided, for the interests of both parties, to govern the disposition of and render convenience to the said forces in and about Korea, and that they shall be determined through mutual agreement between the Republic of Korea and the United States of America acting as the Unified Command in accordance with "The Resolution on the Settlement of the Unified Command" of the Security Council of the United Nations of July 7, 1950. A practical and effective Administrative Agreement to be concluded between the said two parties will help minimize misunderstanding and maximize cooperativeness between the Korean people and United Nations forces personnel in Korea.

In the belief that a conclusion of the Agreement is in the mutual interests, I wish to propose formally, on behalf of the Government of the Republic of Korea, that negotiation will be commenced between the representatives of Korean Government and the United States Government. Upon the receipt of your consent, we will proceed to decide the date and place of the conference, which will be mutually agreeable.

Accept, dear Mr. Chargé d'Affaires, the assurances of my highest consideration.

Enclosure: Draft of Administrative Agreement

Y. T. Pyun
Minister of Foreign Affairs

The Honourable Carl W. Strom,
Chargé d'Affaires,
Embassy of the United States of America
Seoul, Korea

0076

58

57-3-14

57 - 3 - 6 　　　　　　　　　　　　　　　　미문80-1

0077

A N N E X B.

January 5, 1957

Excellency:

I have the honour to refer to the Foreign Minister's note addressed to Mr. Carl W. Strom, Chargé d'Affairs ad interim of the Embassy of the United States of America in Korea dated April 28, 1955 enclosing a draft of an Administrative Agreement between the Republic of Korea and the Unified Command for establishment of the Status of the United Nations Forces in Korea.

In the afore-said note, the Minister informed the Government of the United States of America of the desire of the Korean Government to commence negotiations with the United States Government for the said Status of Forces Agreement which will also define the former's customs functions as referred to in my letter of December 2, 1954.

To this proposal, however, no acceptance has been given as yet, although the American Chargé d'Affairs notified in his replying note of May 9, 1955, that upon obtaining his Government's view on the said request, he would communicate with the Minister.

I hereby wish again to propose, on behalf of my Government, that negotiation be commenced at an earliest possible date between the representatives of the Korean Government and the United States Government. In connection with this re-proposal, I would like further to refer to the note of July 26, 1955 addressed to the Foreign Minister by General Lemnitzer advising on this matter.

/General Lemnitzer

His Excellency
The right honourable
Walter C. Dowling
Ambassador of the United States of
America to the Republic of Korea
Seoul, Korea

0078

59

57-3-15

71-3-6 마-문 80-1

0079

General Lemnitzer expressed his views on the possibility of negotiating the said agreement in the above note to the effect that the United States Government envisages difficulties in commencing immediately negotiations for a proposed agreement for the following two reasons:

The one reason was that it would be preferable to the American Government that negotiations for a proposed treaty of Friendship, Commerce and Navigation between the two countries as well as an agreement guaranteeing investments be completed before the initiation of negotiation for an agreement in question. The other was that the Unified Command cannot participate in negotiation of such agreement without the prior consent of allies within the Unified Command and it is anticipated that the task of obtaining such consent will be difficult.

Attention, however, is paid to the fact that the points indicated above constitute no longer difficulties about negotiating the said agreement under the present circumstances.

The Treaty of Friendship, Commerce and Navigation has been already signed and is now waiting to be formally ratified. As regards the agreement guaranteeing investments, discussions have been completed on provisions of its draft and now the work of finalising it remains only. On the other hand, since allies within the Unified Command have been decreased in number into twelve nations and since the American forces form the predominant components of the United Nations Forces, there exist no difficulties, it is believed, in securing consent of other allies as to the matter.

And thus, even in case the consent of the other allies has not been obtained as yet, it is, therefore, proposed that

/negotiations

-60-

0080
57-3-16

57-3-6

마문P0-1

0081

negotiations be started first between both representatives of the Korean Government and the United States Government and that negotiations with other allies shall be carried on separately in accordance with terms to be agreed upon between Korea and the United States of America. It is sincerely requested that the concurrence of the United States Government be given to the wish of the Korean Government to commence negotiations for the agreement proposed.

Please accept, Excellency, the renewed assurances of my highest consideration.

Chung W. Cho
Minister of
Foreign Affairs

57-3-6 마-문P0-1

0083

ANNEX C.

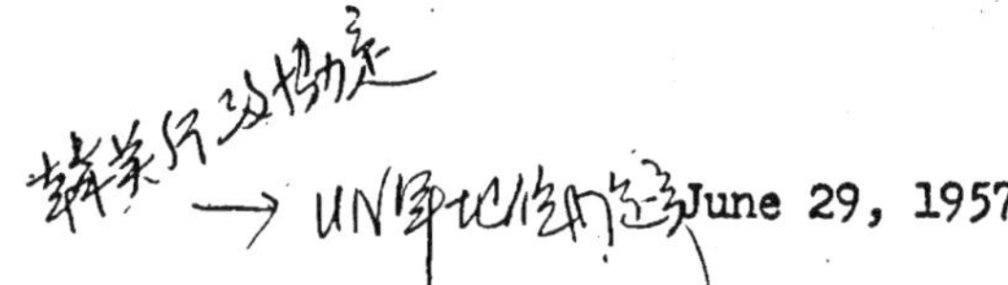

June 29, 1957

My dear Mr. Ambassador:

I have the honor to remind your Government, as I have orally mentioned to you on several occasions, that the conclusion of an Administrative Agreement defining and setting forth in detail the status of United States troops stationed in Korea is still pending.

On April 28, 1955, our draft proposal of an Administrative Agreement between this Government and the Unified Command, to establish the status of United Nations forces in Korea, was addressed to your Embassy. On November 1, 1956, it was proposed that a separate agreement be negotiated between representatives of this Government and the United States Government, in case of difficulty in obtaining early consent of the other Allied Governments.

In the absence of such an administrative agreement, a temporary agreement was made through the exchange of Notes at Taejon, on July 12, 1950, concerning the exclusive jurisdiction by court-martial of the United States over members of the United States Military Establishment in Korea. This agreement, which is still in force, was improvised to meet an emergency situation and is not considered sufficient to meet effectively all the complex and complicated problems arising from the presence of United States troops in Korea

/This Government

His Excellency
Ambassador Walter C. Dowling
American Embassy,
Seoul.

0084

~~62~~ 57-3-18

57-3-6 미·문 PO-1

0085

This Government is strongly convinced that the early conclusion of a formal and detailed agreement on the status of United States troops in Korea would serve to strengthen cordial relations between our people and American military personnel, and would provide great satisfaction to the mutual cause and interest of both countries.

I wish to state again that this Government is most desirous of receiving the concurrence of the United States Government in order to commence negotiations for an administrative agreement along the lines of the proposal of April, 1955. Your Government's earliest favorable consideration of this matter is most sincerely desired.

Accept, Excellency, renewed assurances of my highest consideration.

Chung W. Cho
Minister

0086

~~63~~

57-3-18

57-3-6 미문 70-1

0087

ANNEX D.

韓美行政協定 (SOFA). → 軍隊地位.

26 July 1955

Dear Minister Pyun:

Thank you very much for your letter of 13 June 1955, in which you acknowledge receipt of General Taylor's letter of 14 May 1955, with the inclosures pertaining to customs functions of the Republic of Korea.

I have noted the desire of the Korean Government to commence negotiations with the Government of the United States for a Status of Forces Agreement between the Korean Government and the Unified Command. This matter is presently under study by the Departments of my government in Washington.

Current thinking on this matter is that it would be preferable that negotiations now in progress or pending be completed before the initiation of negotiations for an agreement of the type in question. Ambassador Lacy advises me that a proposed treaty of friendship, commerce and navigation between our respective governments is under consideration, as well as an agreement guaranteeing investments, and that he is anxious to complete these matters before taking up any other major negotiations.

I am sure you are also aware that the Unified Command cannot participate in a negotiation of any Status of Forces Agreement without the prior consent of our allies within the United Nations Command. It is anticipated that the task of obtaining this consent will be difficult and time consuming.

Sincerely,

/s/
L. L. LEMNITZER
General, United States Army
Commander-in-Chief

His Excellency Pyun Yung-Tai
Minister for Foreign Affairs of
The Republic of Korea

~~64~~ 0088

57-3-20

57-3-6 (11)

마문 80-1(11)

0089

가. 주둔군지위협정 교섭

분야별 개별협정 체결방식 수락용의를 표명한 국무부 공한의 Dowling 주한미대사앞 서한 (57.11.13)

Foreign Minister to United States Ambassador

November 13, 1957

Dear Mr. Ambassador:

I wish to bring to your attention the question of an Agreement on the status of the United States Forces in Korea and to recent developments in our efforts to solve problems arising between members of the United States Forces and Korean nationals.

Since the cessation of active hostilities in 1953, it has become increasingly clear that a *modus vivendi* reached between our two Governments through an exchange of notes at Taejon on July 12, 1950 allowing the United States exclusive jurisdiction by court-martial of members of the United States Forces in Korea is not sufficient to cope with various complicated problems involving members of the United States Forces and our people.

This Government, keenly desiring to conclude an agreement on the status of United States Forces in our Country, initially proposed to your Government through the Foreign Minister's note of April 28, 1955, that negotiations be commenced for that purpose, and later, having failed to receive any positive reaction to this proposal, brought up the matter again on several occasions. When the Under Secretary of State visited Korea, a note on this question dated September 10, 1957, was presented to Mr. Herter in the hope that

0090-1

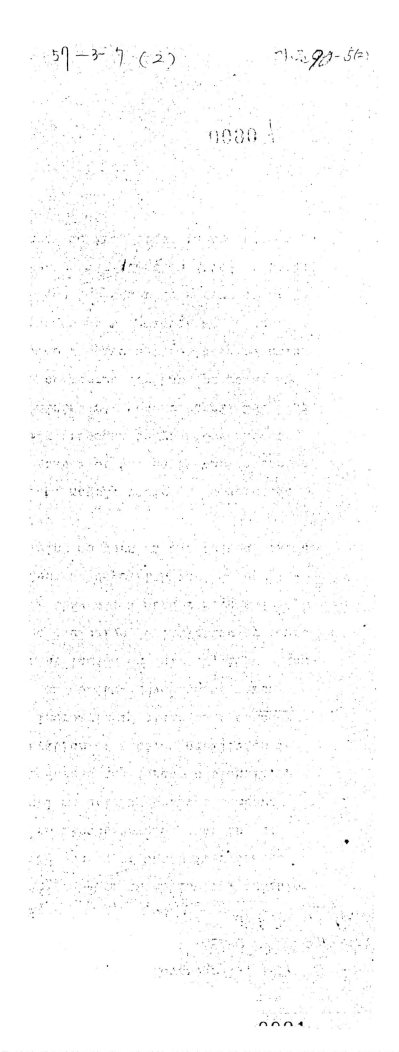

the matter would receive his favorable attention. A copy of this note is enclosed.

In this connection, I am deeply interested in a suggestion made by you at a meeting held in my office on October 10 1957 that "there might be room for reaching a separate agreement on particular items as was done in the utilities problems" I deeply appreciate your friendly and cooperative interest in these problems and will be very happy to proceed with negotiations for separate agreements with your Government on particular items; for instance, taxation, customs duty, and criminal jurisdiction. I am confident such negotiations will lead to an acceptable solution to our common problems.

With warmest personal regards, I remain,

Sincerely yours,

Chung W. Cho
Minister

His Excellency
Walter C. Dowling
Ambassador,
American Embassy,
Seoul

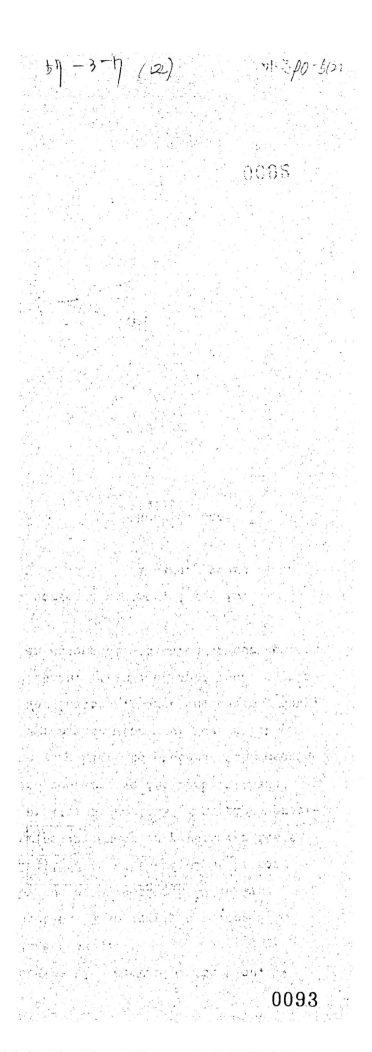

Recommendation on Seperate Agreements between Korea and the United States regarding the Status of the United States forces

Considering the present deadlock between Korea and the United States regarding the commencement of negotiations for the conclusion of an full-scaled administrative agreement to govern entire status of the United States forces in Korea, it is recommended to conclude between the two governments under-mentioned several agreements seperately so that the status of the United States forces in Korea can be regulated as far as possible upon mutually acceptable basis:

1) Agreement concerning Procurement, Taxation and Custom Duties of United States forces in Korea (Ref. Art. 6, 7, 8, 9 of Draft Administrative Agreement proposed by the Korean Government);

2) Agreement concerning Settlement of Claims relative to the stationing of United States forces in Korea (Art. 5);

3) Agreement concerning Entry and Exit of United States forces in Korea (Art. 2)

4) Agreement concerning Facilities and Areas to be used by the United States forces in Korea (Art. 3, para. 10 of Art. 4)

5) Agreement concerning Criminal Jurisdiction over Offences by the United States forces in Korea (Art. 4, 13, 14).

For the general provisions, each agreement will contain commonly such clauses as on Expression of Terms, Uniforms and Markings, Measures in the Events of Hostilities, Joint Committee, Coming into Force, Revision, and, Validity and Suspension. (Ref. Art. 1, 12, 15, 16, 17, 18, 19)

1. Agreement concerning Procurement, Taxation and Customs Duties of United States forces in Korea.

It is vital for ~~the part of~~ the Republic of Korea to prevent and crack down the sumuggling conducted through the supply route of the United States forces in Korea. This agreement is one of the most urgent agreements to be concluded between the two countries. For the purpose of preventing and checking the aforesaid smuggling, the Korean Customs Officials should have opportunity to access to and supervise the wharves and military airports which are now exclusively held and controled by the United States military authorities,

0094

As for procurement, due consideration should be made so that such procurements may bring about no adverse effect upon Korean economy.

2. Agreement concerning Settlement of Claims relative to the United States forces in Korea

This Agreement is to govern the civil jurisdiction, particularly the settlement of claims arising out of injuries and damages. This agreement is aimed to clarify the responsibility of the injuries of and damages to the Korean nationals and their properties caused by the United States forces, and to facilitate settlement of the claims arising out of such injuries and damages. On the other hand, the Korean Government will undertake to make efforts to protect the United States forces and their members from the injuries of and damages to their bodies and properties.

3. Agreement concerning Entry and Exit of United States forces in Korea.

This agreement will clarify the scope of exemption from Korean immigration laws and regulations for the members of the United States forces including the civilian component and their dependents, thus minimizing smuggling or stowaway cases.

4. Agreement concerning Facilities and Areas to be used by the United States forces in Korea.

While the Korean Government is willing to grant to the United States forces the use of certain facilities and areas and some kinds of rights, power and authory, necessary for carrying out their mission, this agreement is aimed to clarify the scope of exemption from the liabilities of compensation or restoration accruing from the use of such facilities and areas.

This agreement will also contain provisions regulating the military post offices and non-appropriated fund organizations, and further such provisions as enabling the Government to make interim use of such facilities or areas as target ranges or maneuver grounds which are temporarily not used by the United States forces.

5. Agreement concerning Criminal Jurisdiction over Offences by the United States forces in Korea.

Since it seems that the United States Government is very reluctant to conclude such an agreement, it is thought unwise to propose to the United States Government to commence negotiations for concluding an entirely new agreement in this regard despite the existance of the so called Taejon Agreement concluded in 1950 by exchange of notes which provides for exclusive jurisdiction of U.S. court-marshal over the members of/United States forces. It is, therefore, recommended to suggest the United States Government to amend the aforesaid existing agreement so as to suit the conditions changed since the cessation of actual hostilities. As for the amendment, efforts should be made to limit the jurisdiction of the United States court-marshal over the members of the United States forces to such cases as occured in the course of execution of official duties, and further to make additional provisions for judicial cooperation including joint search and investigation.

0096

57 SOFA

9.

57.12.3. 미대사대리의 11.26자 아측 각서 접수확인서한

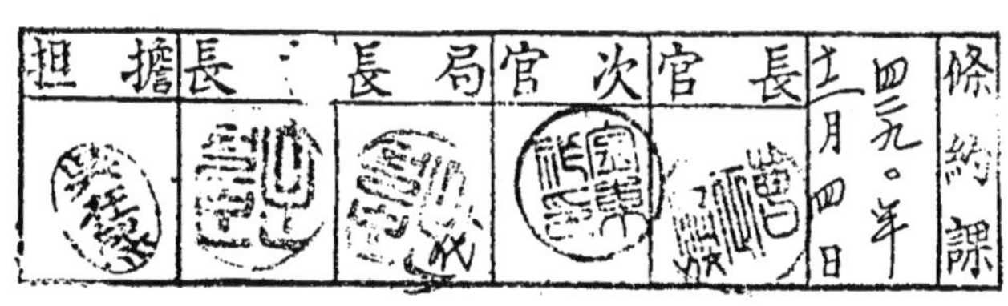

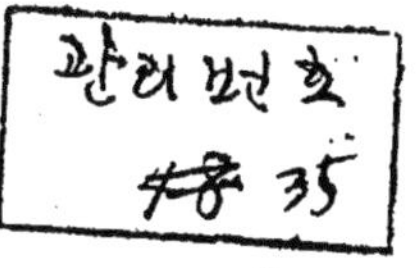

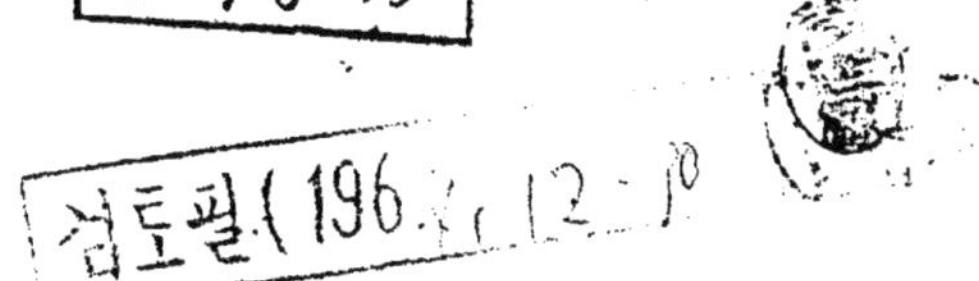

American Embassy,
Seoul, Korea,
December 3, 1957.

My dear Mr. Minister:

I have the honor to acknowledge receipt of your letter of November 26, 1957 with which was enclosed a memorandum concerning the position of your Government on the question of negotiating separate agreements on various subjects pertaining to the status of United States forces in Korea.

I have forwarded copies of your letter and enclosure to Washington for consideration by my Government.

I shall hope, in due course, to send you a further communication on the subject of your Government's memorandum.

With warmest personal regards, I am

Sincerely yours,

T. Eliot Weil

T. Eliot Weil
Charge d'Affaires ad interim

His Excellency
Chung W. Cho,
Minister of Foreign Affairs,
Republic of Korea.

0097-1

to K.M.D.

Explanation on the Military Post Office
and non-Appropriate Fund Organizations
to be regulated by the Separate Agreement

과도문류로인사여
영변문이로 재분류
1962. 2. 16.

As for the military post office and non-appropriated fund organizations, the full-scale draft agreement ~~on the status of~~ United Nations forces between Korea and the ~~Unified Command~~ proposed by the Korean Government to the Uni~~ted States Government~~ contains provisions regarding the military post office and non-appropriated fund organizations such as navy exchanges, post exchanges, messes, social clubs, theaters and newspapers. It is intended that the substance of the above-mentioned provisions, that is Articles 9 and 10 of the draft agreement, be included in the seperate agreement to be concluded between the two Governments. The provisions of Articles 9 and 10 of the draft agreement is attached hereto. Since the memorandum to be forwarded to the American Embassy is purported to indicate only essential points to be included in the separate agreements and since the position of the Korean Government on how to regulate the matters is already expressed in the draft agreement referred to in the above, it is considered appropriate to point out in the memorandum only the subjects to be regulated by the separate agreement.

0098

Draft Administrative ~~Agreement regarding~~
the Status of the United Nations Forces
proposed by the Korean Government to
the United States Government.

과는분류로 인하여
일반문서로 재분류
1962. 2. 17.

Article IX

1. (a) Navy exchanges, post exchanges, messes, social clubs, theaters, newspapers and other non-appropriated funds organizations authorized and regulated by the United Nations forces authorities may be established in the facilities and areas in use by the United Nations forces for the use of members of such forces, the civilian component, and their dependents. Except as otherwise provided in this Agreement, such organizations shall not be subject to Korean regulations, license, fees, taxes or similar controls.

(b) When a newspaper authorized and regulated by the United Nations forces authorities is sold to the general public, it shall be subject to Korean regulations, license, fees, taxes or similar controls so far as such circulation is concerned.

2. No Korean tax shall be imposed on sales of merchandise and services by such organizations, except as provided in paragraph 1 (b) of this Article, but purchases within Korea of merchandise and supplies by such organizations shall be subject to Korean taxes.

3. Except as such disposal may be authorized by the Korean and the United Nations forces authorities in accordance with mutually

0099

agreed conditions, goods which are sold by such organizations shall not be disposed of in Korea to persons not authorized to make purchases from such organizations.

4. The organizations referred to in this Article shall provide such information to the Korean authorities as is required by Korean legislations.

Article X

The United Command shall have the right to establish and operate, within the facilities and areas in use by the United Nations forces, the United Nations forces military post offices for the use of members of the United Nations forces, the civilian component and their dependents, for the transmission of mail between the United Nations forces military post offices in Korea and between such military post offices and their home states post offices.

일반문서로 재분류
(협정 체결시)

0100

1959.4.3.

SOFA 관계

주한미군 사용시설과 구역에 관한 협정 체결 교섭 개시를
제의하는 국무부 장관의
Dowling 주한 미대사앞 공한

April 3, 1959

My dear Ambassador:

I have the honor of writing to you regarding a conclusion of an agreement concerning the facilities and areas to be used by the United States Forces in Korea.

For years, there existed a strong opinion among our people and the Government of the Republic of Korea that an agreement concerning the facilities and areas to be used by the United States Forces in Korea be concluded, because our people and the Government fear that our good relations may be obviously affected in the absence of an agreement that defines in detail as to under what terms the facilities and areas be granted to them. I believe that these terms could be covered if our two Governments conclude an agreement on Status of Forces as our Government proposed in 1954. But pending such proposal, an agreement on the subject as stated above would mark a step forward in the direction of the settlement of the problems between the two Governments.

Therefore, I wish to propose formally, on behalf of the Korean Government, that negotiation be commenced between the representatives of my Government and the United States for the agreement proposed.

His Excellency
The right honorable
Walter C. Dowling

59-18-1 (2)

미.관 PO-10(2)

agreement proposed./

0104

Upon the receipt of your consent, we shall appoint our representatives, and shall also suggest a date and place of the conference which will be mutually agreeable.

Accept, my dear Ambassador, the assurances of my highest consideration.

Sincerely yours,

Chung W. Cho
Minister
of Foreign Affairs
Republic of Korea

CP-18-2

0103

0104

Foreign Minister to the United States Ambassador

June 10, 1959

Excellency,

I have the honor to draw your attention to the subject of usage of the facilities and areas now in use by the U.S. forces in Korea.

As you may recall, most of the facilities and areas presently in use by the U.S. forces in Korea were furnished by the Korean authorities under the emergency state during and immediately after the outbreak of the Korean War. Under the then prevailing situation, no adequate agreement was concluded between the Government of the Republic of Korea and the Government of the United States of America to regulate various problems in relation to these facilities.

My Government feels that it would best serve the interests of both countries that are wholeheartedly engaged in their joint efforts against the common enemy if the two Governments conclude an equitable agreement regarding the same. In view of the fact that the absence of such an agreement in the past made it impossible to resolve problems related to the use of such facilities and areas, an agreement of this nature would improve the defense efforts of the two Governments.

His Excellency
Walter C. Dowling
Ambassador of the United States of
America

0105

I wish to propose, therefore, that the representatives of both the Korean and U.S. Government meet and discuss and later conclude such an agreement which could cover ~~(1)~~ regulations to enable the United States forces in Korea to carry out their operation in a most effective way; (2) set out the conditions under which the U.S. forces will be using the facilities and areas involved; (3) with the Korean Government granting, in accordance with international precedents, the continued use by the United States forces of such facilities and areas and (4) with the United States Government giving full consideration to owners of the properties.

I sincerely hope that the above will receive favorable consideration by your Government and that discussions could be commenced at the earliest date possible with end in view of concluding an agreement along the lines indicated above, without delay.

Accept, Excellency, the renewed assurances of my highest consideration.

Chung W. Cho
Minister

United States Ambassador to Foreign Minister

No. 983 Seoul, June 15, 1959.

Excellency:

I have the honor to refer to Your Excellency's note of June 10, 1959, proposing negotiation and conclusion of an agreement on the usage of facilities and areas now in use by United States Forces in Korea.

I also have the honor to inform Your Excellency that I have forwarded your proposal to the Department of State for its consideration.

Accept, Excellency, the renewed assurances of my highest consideration.

협정체결서 일반문서로 재분류

/s/
Walter C. Dowling

His Excellency
Cho Chong-hwan,
Minister of Foreign Affairs,
Seoul.

0109

60. 3. 31.

외무차관과 주한미대사간의

한일관계 언급시 등 [illegible]

REPORT KPO / 154

March 31, 1960

TO : His Excellency the President

FROM : Vice Foreign Minister

SUBJECT : Initial Report on the Meeting with Ambassador McConaughy

Vice Foreign Minister Kyu Hah Choi had an exclusive meeting with U.S. Ambassador Walter P. McConaughy at Bando Hotel for about an hour from 3:00 p.m., March 30, 1960.

1. Ambassador McConaughy delivered a note which is a reply to the Ministry's letter of June 10, 1959, proposing to commence negotiations for concluding an agreement on the use of facilities and areas by the U.S. Forces in Korea. The Ministry will submit its observation and recommendation thereon separately.

2. Ambassador McConaughy briefed on the Baguio Conference of U.S. Diplomats in Asia. He said that the American diplomats in Asia reviewed overall picture of the area of the past decade and studied the prospect for the future decade. According to Ambassador McConaughy, the American diplomats saw some progress in the area but found no ground for "complacency". They recommended to the U.S. Government that efforts to resist Communist threat in this area and to keep the MSA programs at the present level be redoubled, so that the Secretary of State may use their recommendation when testifying before the U.S. Congress which might contend to reduce

10-1

0110-1

aids to this area. He also stated that the conferees reaffirmed the present U.S. policy of not recognizing Communist China. Details of his briefing on the Baguio Conference will be submitted separately.

3. Ambassador McConaughy touched upon the Korea-Japan relations and stated that he was "heartened" to see the exchange of detainees effected between the two Governments.

Vice-Foreign Minister Choi, pointing out the fact that the deportation is being carried out by the Japanese side, urged that the United States and free world should realize the deportation is conducted with the assistance of Russia and that the United States will do something to cope with the situation.

Most respectfully,

Enclosure: copy of U.S. note under reference

0113

American Embassy,

Seoul, March 30, 1960.

No. 2391

Excellency:

I have the honor to refer to former Foreign Minister Cho's note of June 10, 1959, and to Your Excellency's note of October 15, 1959, in which reference was made to a proposal of the Government of the Republic of Korea for the negotiation of an agreement on the use of facilities and areas by United States military forces in Korea.

On behalf of my government I am pleased to accept your proposal for the initiation of negotiations on a Facilities and Areas Agreement subject to the following mutual understandings:

(1) that a revision of the arrangements set forth in the notes exchanged between our two governments at Taejon on July 12, 1950, will not be proposed by either side; and (2) that compensation to the owners or suppliers of any real property in Korea which has been or will be used by the United States Armed Forces in the responsibility of the Korean Government.

Upon receipt of Your Excellency's acknowledgment that these understandings are acceptable to the Korean Government, the United States Government will be pleased to undertake discussions on the proposed Facilities and Areas Agreement.

Accept, Excellency, the renewed assurances of my highest consideration.

His Excellency
Choi Kyu Hah,
Acting Minister for Foreign Affairs,
Seoul.

0114

159 March 31, '60

SUBJECT : Summary Record of Conversation with Ambassador McConaughy

Vice Foreign Minister Kyu Hah Choi had a meeting with U.S. Ambassador Walter P. McConaughy, at the latter's request, at Bando Hotel for about an hour from 3:00 p.m., March 30, 1960. The following is the gist of conversation which took place at the above meeting.

I. Ambassador McConaughy handed a note to Vice Foreign Minister Choi, which is in reply to the Ministry's letter of June 10, 1959 requesting the U.S. Government to commence negotiations for conclusion of an agreement on the facilities and areas now in use by the U.S. forces in Korea. A copy of the above U.S. note was submitted to the Office of the President on March 30, 1960 (KPO-154).

II. Ambassador McConaughy turned to the Baguio Conference of American Diplomats in Asia. According to Ambassador McConaughy, U.S. diplomats stationed in Asian countries held a similar conference at Bangkok in 1950. The Baguio Conference, therefore, was held to review the overall picture in the area of the past decade and to study the prospect of the future decade.

Generally speaking, Mr. McConaughy said, the American diplomats at the Baguio Conference felt that crises in Asia were overcome to certain extent and situation in the region is better now than it was in 1950. The following are resume of views held by conferees as told by Ambassador McConaughy:

9-1

0115

0116

Taiwan: Taiwan is a show-case of economic stability.

The Philippines: In the Philippines, the Huks were suppressed and the government is stable and definitely on the free nations' side.

Burma: Burma, which used to be an ultra-neutral country, became more cooperative toward the free nations and situation there is secure.

Thailand: Situation is stable in Thailand.

Indonesia: Indonesia is in lack of stability both in political and economic fields but her relations with the United States are better than before.

Vietnam: The Republic of Vietnam registered more progress than that achieved by Communist Vietminh.

Cambodia: Cambodia turned more toward neutralism but she is not a Communist country yet.

Laos: Laos is a big question mark, but Communist efforts in Laos were repelled at least for the time being.

(Ambassador McConaughy deliberately evaded any comment on Korea.)

Ambassador McConaughy stated that the conferees at the Baguio Conference felt that they should be gratified to see some progress attained by countries in the area. They, however, recognized that there is no ground for "complacency". In the view of the U.S. diplomats attending the Baguio Conference, Communist threat to this area is greater than ever before. They were particularly disturbed by the military and economic potentiality of Communist China. They

9 - 2

0118

were particularly disturbed by the military and economic potentiality of Communist China. They recognized the need to redouble the U.S. efforts to meet the danger posed by Communist China.

Some U.S. Congressmen may try to reduce the size of military and economic aids to this area in next series of years, but the U.S. diplomats thought that it was based on "mistaken" assumption. They, therefore, wrote to Secretary of State, emphasizing the danger still existing in this area, so that he may use this point of view when testifying before the Congress. The following are main points of the said letter (Mr. McConaughy briefed using a four-page letter):

In Asia which has a population of 800-millions, Japan is the only major industrial country for free world security. In this area, situation in generally speaking more encouraging than a year ago, but U.S. mutual security programs are still needed as essential means of resisting such Communist danger by the people in the area and as vital supplement to their own efforts in the region which is vulnerable to Communist invasion. Ambassador McConaughy stated that Korea is listed at the top of the list of such countries.

The American diplomats stressed the necessity of offering continued economic aid (for defense support), technical assistance, DLF programs, etc. to the countries of the region. They believed that their letter would be used by Secretary Herter in his explanation to the Congress when foreign aid question

9-3

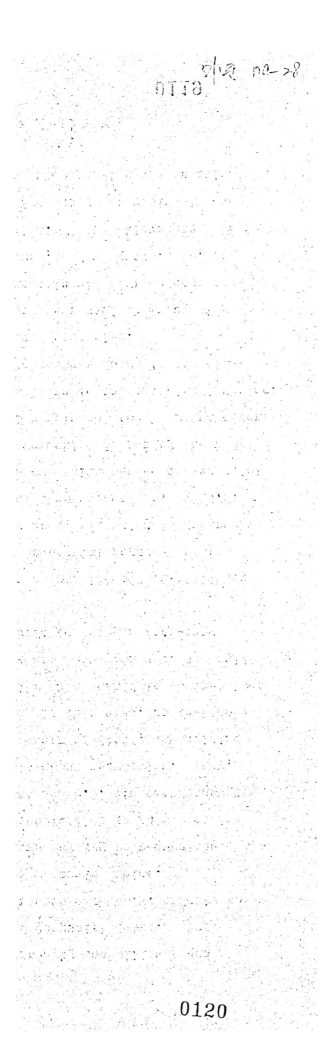

should undergo heavy fire of Congressional debate.

The conferees submitted a conclusion and recommendation, which part is classified as secret. For confidential information, Ambassador McConaughy confided to the Vice Foreign Minister the followings:

In general, there was noted a progress in the Far Eastern countries. The conferees noted that the nature of the present Communist threat is less dramatic. Japan constitutes a considerable element of free nations strength. In Indonesia, there exists economic and political instability and no settlement is in sight at the present stage. The U.S. diplomats felt relieved as they noted that the Communist insurgency is removed. Thailand is considered as a corner stone of U.S. foreign policy in this area. In conclusion, the conferees thought that the past decade was spent mainly for national survival to maintain internal security and political integrity.

Communist China's threat to the region is not only military but also economic. Except Japan and the Republic of China, no great economic progress is noted in the region. Indonesia made retreat in the field of economy. The conferees anticipated that the population of Asia in next decade will increase up to 2-billions. They expressed fear that Communist China might become leading power in Asia in the field of technology. As witnessed in Tibetan and Indian border incidents, there is an increasing threat from Communist China. Peiping seems to have no interest at all even in concluding a _modus vivendi_ with the United States. They agreed

9-4

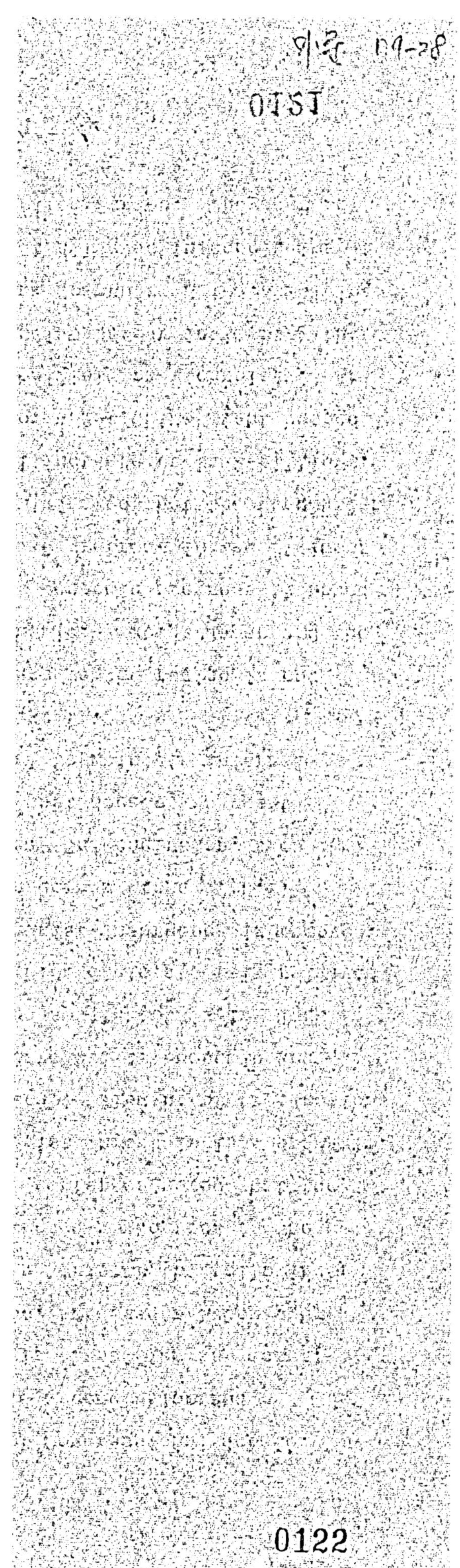

that the so-called two-China policy is not acceptable. This point was well enunciated in the speech of Assistant Secretary of State Parsons at Wisconsin on February 19, 1960, in which he reemphasized the firm stand against Red China. The United States conducted talks with Red China at Panmoonjum, Geneva and Warsaw, but this is distinctly separated from the question of recognizing Red China. Ambassador McConaughy said that the U.S. will continue its policy to recognize Free China (Republic of China) and to reject Communist China. The Sino-Russian relations are more cohesive than diversive and it would be a serious mistake if one assumes that there is any significant cleavage in Sino-Russian relations. The American diplomats reaffirmed the necessity for the U.S. to maintain close relations with the Republic of China and also the necessity of keeping a big standing army in Formosa.

Urgent problems which Indonesia is confronted with now are how to obtain technical and monetary aids. Generally speaking, the U.S. is better understood by countries in the Far East than a decade ago, but the U.S. should be consistent in meeting the aggression to this area. Mr. McConaughy stated that Nationalism is growing in this area, which the U.S. diplomats concluded, is a good tendency because Nationalism is opposed by Communism.

The American diplomats admitted that the Soviet success in the field of space science resulted in an increased prestige for Soviet Russia among the Asians

9-5

0124

and in this respect, the U.S. suffered a setback. The conferees recognized the necessity for the U.S. to be prepared for the possibility of limited war and the necessity of keeping U.S. ground forces at the present level. They also felt the necessity of keeping economic and military aids to the countries of the region at the present level. In meeting Asian demand for better life, the U.S. must encourage free institutions and free enterprises. The conferees recognized the important role of European countries in the economic development of Far Eastern countries and felt it necessary that European countries should co-operate with the U.S. in this project. They also recognized the responsibility of Japan in participating in this economic development program.

As for Okinawa, the American diplomats agreed that the island should be placed under exclusive U.S. administration for the time being. They saw no state of democracy is deeply rooted in Asian countries, while admitting that the democratic institution in this area does not necessarily have to be a Western-styled one in view of its own environment. They recognized, however, that democracy does not survive in the state of insecurity or backwardness. There is no distinct tendency of "regionalism" in the Far East except the case of SEATO. Economic regionalism has many difficulties and it is felt necessary that efforts through ECAFE and cooperation by the United States be sought to attain economic stability in the region. In this regard, the conferees found it advisable that

9 - 6

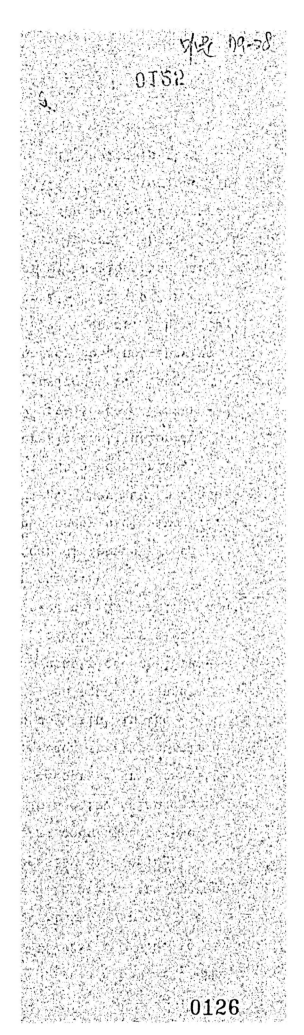

exchange programs of Fulbright-type or Leaders Grant-type be continued. Ambassador McConaughy pointed out that no Fulbright program is operated in Korea.

The U.S. future security and well being is heavily dependent upon this area, and the U.S. should demonstrate that they are acting on firm conviction. Survival is an elementary question but this was the major problem in Asia of the last decade.

III. Ambassador McConaughy then touched upon the Korea-Japan problems. On his way back to Seoul from Baguio, he said he dropped in Tokyo. He talked with Ambassador MacArthur in Tokyo and they were both heartened to see that mutual exchange of detainees was effected between Korea and Japan. He said that he was told that the Japanese side was watching attentively the attitude of the Korean Government as to whether or not it would repatriate to Japan those Japanese fishermen who shall have served out their sentences as of April 9, 1960, and later on.

Vice Foreign Minister Choi stated that we are carefully watching, too, how far Japan would go on with the detainees issue. He said that the discussion on March 19, 1960 was on those Japanese fishermen who had served out their sentences as of that date and that future development depends on sincerity on Japan's part.

Ambassador McConaughy said that he knew very well of the Korean feeling on the detainees issue and the seriousness of the effect in case the so-called Calcutta Agreement should be extended. He deplored

9-7 0127

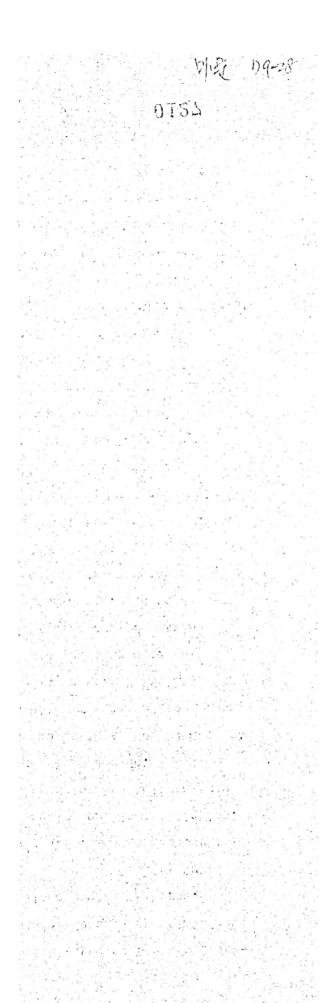

0130

the fact that the active propaganda and brain-washing activities by the Communist CHORYUN are quiet effective.

Vice Foreign Minister Choi stated that the Free World including the United States should be awakened to the seriousness of Japan's continuance of deportation scheme and urged that the something should be done to stop this scheme by the United States.

9 - 8 0129

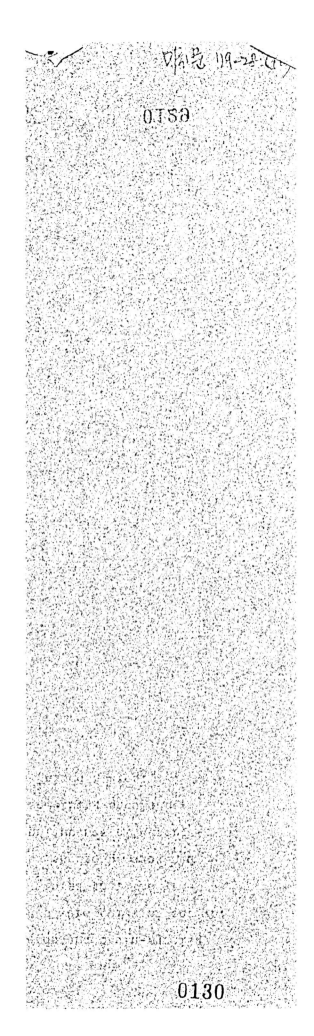

(駐美大使에게 보낸 것)

APR - 6 1960

SUBJECT : Ministry's observation on the U.S. note regarding proposed agreement on the facilities and areas in use by U.S. forces in Korea

In reply to a proposal made by our Government on June 10, 1959 for commencement of negotiations to conclude an agreement on the facilities and areas in use by United States forces in Korea, U.S. Ambassador McConaughy handed a note to Vice-Foreign Minister Choi, according to which the United States would accept our proposal on the following "understandings":

1) that a revision of the arrangements set forth in the notes exchanged between our two governments at Taejon on July 12, 1950, will not be proposed by either side; and

2) that compensation to the owners or suppliers of any real property in Korea which has been or will be used by the United States Armed Forces is the responsibility of the Korean Government.

In the view of the Ministry:

1) The U.S. position on item 1 of the above understandings is a similar one which then-American Ambassador Dowling under instructions from Washington informally suggested on September 18, 1958 to the former Vice-Foreign Minister. (KPO/101 dated September 18 1958) According to Ambassador Dowling at that time, the United States would enter negotiation for status of forces agreement of "purely administrative nature," unless it touches upon the problem of criminal jurisdiction. This suggestion was hardly acceptable to us. Significance of the latest U.S. proposal is that the previous U.S. view which had been informally delivered was set forth in a formal note; and

2) With regard to the problem of compensation

0131

-0132

to be paid to owners or suppliers of any real property, if this U.S. condition be accepted, any agreement which may be reached on that basis would bear only a token of significance on our part.

Under the circumstances, the settlement of problems on the basis of the U.S. proposed conditions would achieve something but would result in concluding the long-pending question concerning criminal jurisdiction against our favor. This will not convince our people.

0133

외고문서 비밀해제: 주한미군지위협정(SOFA) 16
주한미군지위협정(SOFA) 서명 및 발효 16

초판인쇄 2024년 03월 15일
초판발행 2024년 03월 15일

지은이 한국학술정보(주)
펴낸이 채종준
펴낸곳 한국학술정보(주)
주 소 경기도 파주시 회동길 230(문발동)
전 화 031-908-3181(대표)
팩 스 031-908-3189
홈페이지 http://ebook.kstudy.com
E-mail 출판사업부 publish@kstudy.com
등 록 제일산-115호(2000. 6. 19)

ISBN 979-11-7217-027-1 94340
979-11-7217-011-0 94340 (set)